Strategic Internet Marketing

The Authoritative Internet Marketing Guide for Legal Professionals

Attract more clients, dominate your local geographic area, eliminate the stress of marketing your services and leverage your business for all that it's worth!
Enjoy more freedom, money, and time!

Cheryl Waller, BSB/MKT, MBA

SIMCcorp.com
SIMC Corp

SIMC

© 2015 by SIMC Corp and Cheryl Waller

Printed in the USA

Published by SIMC Publishing Services, Vero Beach, FL
SIMCpublishing.com

Some Hand-Drawn Graphics Provided By David Imperato
Editing By Lee Kindig
Editing By Jeff Reynolds
Editing By Megan Patterson

ISBN: 0692453792
ISBN-13: 978-0692453797

DEDICATION

This book is dedicated to the memory of my daughter Julia, to my boys (Michael, Bryan, Nicholas), to my granddaughter Aubrielle, to my fiancé Daniel, and to my awesome team members at SIMC Corp.

I also dedicate this book to you. The pages you are about to read will transform your business and personal life if you diligently apply the strategies in this book to your business.

Always remember that the key to marketing success is **SIMC:** *(Strategy, Implementation, Magnetism, and Consistency)*

Cheryl Waller

AS SEEN ON

CBS NEWS abc MarketWatch From DOW JONES

NBC FOX MERRILL EDGE AP

REUTERS

The Boston Globe

THE CW Newsweek

WALL STREET SELECT

Verification Links: http://strategicimcorp.com/as-seen-on.php

SIMC

Full-Service Clients:	StrategicIMcorp.com
FREE Training:	GoSIMC.com
FREE Reputation Report:	GetMySnapshot.com
Professional Coaching:	BrassBallsUniversity.com
Publicity Advertising:	TheCelebrityMakers.com

Office Hours: 9a – 5p EST Monday – Friday

(866) 986 - 5650 or (772) 237 – 3880

Support@StrategicIMcorp.com

CONTENTS

i.   **Introduction to Internet Marketing**   9
*why we do what we do, whom this book is for,
whom this book is not for, and what you will learn*

1.   **Content Strategy**   27
*how to develop a content marketing strategy for
your website and blog*

2.   **Blogging Strategy**   41
how to use your blog as a traffic magnet

3.   **Traffic Generation Strategy**   65
*drive traffic to your website with time tested and
amazingly effective strategies*

4.   **Competitive SEO Strategy**   77
*how to properly perform search engine optimization
to get on page one of SERPs*

5.   **Website Design Strategy**   93
*how to use website design to make it easier for
humans (and robots) to find the information they
want*

6.   **Responsive Web Design Strategy**   106
*how to use responsive website design, and why it
works so well*

7. **Local Internet Marketing** 123
   *discover the easy ways to get your website ranked in
   top search engine results in your local geographic
   area*

8. **Video Marketing Strategy** 131
   *creating search engine optimized videos that drive
   mass traffic to your site*

9. **Social Media Marketing Strategy** 152
   *using the golden 5 social media to attract and
   maintain loyal clients and turn them into raving fans*

10. **Publicity Advertising Strategy** 173
    *leveraging the news media to spread the word about
    your business through third-party endorsements and
    mentions.*

11. **Putting It All Together With SIMC** 190
    *strategy, implementation, magnetism, and
    consistency*

PAGE INTENTIONALLY BLANK

INTRODUCTION TO STRATEGIC INTERNET MARKETING

I can remember the first time that I realized the power of Internet marketing. I was in my 20s, and in the process of transitioning out of the military. I had started a small business at home, selling everything from video games to electric and motor scooters. I started with a small eBay store (back when eBay was cheap and PayPal was free), and grew the small company into a full-fledged e-commerce business, which grossed $300,000 in its first year. I imported products from all over the world, and ran the entire business from a laptop computer in my kitchen. The company was number one on Google (and dog pile – yes, they are still around today) before number one on Google meant anything to anyone, and I realized that I was seriously on to something. I worked with content on the site to show up for different search terms with astounding results. This all happened years before search engine optimization was even thought of by most people. Heck, most people thought AOL *was* the Internet (remember… "You've got mail!"). I was a geek. My friends thought I was crazy. My family thought I was crazy. I would sit up for 2 or 3 days playing with the site, and watch the numbers climb. Being a "Geek" was paying. In the first year, the company opened a brick-and-mortar location to keep up with the demand. By 2004, I sold the business, and began my romance with Internet marketing.

For several years, I offered Internet marketing services as an SEO, SEM, and SMM consultant to real estate brokers, legal professionals, and small business owners around the world. I worked as a contributing author to several websites, and offered advice on dominating search engine results. For a short time, I worked in the corporate world, but found that my true passion was helping clients individually. The corporate world couldn't care less about the individual small business owner. So, I submitted my resignation, and moved on.

Under my own name, I operated as a freelance business working for professionals on an individual basis. I worked with each person, each client, each company, one at a time and helped them achieve phenomenal results. At the time, I was a single mother raising three boys. So, I limited myself to six clients at a time, and reserved the weekends to spend time with my boys.

There were a few times that I had to fire a client who demanded more of my time than I could (or would) provide. That conversation, however, is for another time. I found it best to maintain clients that appreciated my expertise, and leveraged my skills. You can't always please everyone, and sometimes it's best to let over-demanding clients go. When you are a one-woman-show, it's important to balance your time effectively. Allowing one client to over-burden your business and family life is never healthy. But, over time my two older boys grew up and moved out, and this allowed me to take on more clients on a 'by-referral-only' basis.

In 2013, I incorporated Strategic Internet Marketing Corp, after realizing that the business had outgrown the ability of one person to manage many accounts. I formed teams to better service our clients in different areas of Internet marketing. However, I never lose sight of the danger of becoming an uncaring corporate entity. So, the business maintains the promise of one-point-of-contact for every client. There is no reason why any of our legal professionals should ever have to master the lingo and acronyms (and learn the differences between them), just to be able to market their business on the Internet. We understand that you want more clients, not a degree in methodical online marketing. So, with the help of talented and experienced in-house teams, Strategic Internet Marketing Corp provided luxury package Internet marketing services that made our clients' lives easier, and their businesses busier.

When the company first Incorporated, we Incorporated under the name Strategic Internet Marketing Corp. Over time we shortened this to SIMC in our communications with clients. In early 2015, we began considering a name change for the company. We decided upon SIMC Corp. We wanted to maintain some of the essence of the old name and create something a little more unique that would grow with the company as it expanded to encompass more than just online marketing. SIMC Corp stands for strategy, implementation, magnetism, and consistency. Each of these are core values in the marketing services that we provide for our clients. All marketing must start with a strategy. Nothing will happen for your business unless you implement your strategy. Your marketing must magnetically attract and retain the ideal client for your business. And finally, you must be deliberate and consistent with your marketing efforts. Without SIMC, you have no consistent source of new clients.

The vision of SIMC Corp is to be the largest all-in-one online marketing agency for busy professionals. Our mission is to provide professionals with the online marketing services and advice they need to bring clients to their door. Our teams create a unique brand, marketing strategy, and polished online identity for each client at a fraction of the cost of a full-time employee. Our services allow our clients to concentrate on serving current clients, while we concentrate on the strategic systems that bring them the next client. We change businesses, generate return on investment, build relationships, and deliver outstanding service every day.

We believe that corporate accountability begins with personal accountability and consciously support each other in making positive and ethical decisions. We believe that expertise is static, so we relentlessly embrace opportunities to grow and learn through ongoing education. We think sustainably with the understanding that any one company decision will last longer than any one individual. We appreciate and care for each other, and our clients, as a diverse family. We cherish and respect our environment, our community, and our planet.

Together we combine aggressive online marketing strategies with the most understandable solutions in an open and honest small business relationship. At SIMC Corp we hire educated talent and we work together as a team in the best interest of each individual client.

We offer strategic all-in-one Internet marketing solutions for busy professionals. We take a team approach and focus on your individual marketing strategy. *We do all of this for less than the cost of one full-time employee.*

Think of investing in your business as investing in energy-efficient light bulbs. You can buy a lot of cheap light bulbs and that will 'do the trick' for now. But, when you plan ahead and invest a little extra upfront, then, in the long run, you are saving time, energy and cost.

WHAT SIMC MEANS

Before we changed the name of the company to SIMC Corp, SIMC stood for Strategic Internet Marketing Corp, but as the company evolved, we found that, for our clients, SIMC has a deeper meaning. SIMC stands for Strategy, Implementation, Magnetism and Consistency. These four components together are the most powerful ingredient for successful business marketing on the Internet.

Strategy

Without a strategy, you're doomed from the start. Any smart business owner knows that a successful business is a direct result of planning. If you do not plan your Internet marketing strategy, then you do not have a chance of reaching your potential client. This is not something that you leave to your 19-year-old nephew in creating your website, or to your assistant who is supposed to be taking care of other tasks. It's important that you hire a professional to create an Internet marketing strategy that will work specifically for your company.

Implementation

Implementation is the most important part of SIMC. If you do not implement your strategy, *then why create one at all?* Simple as that.

Magnetism

In order for your strategy to work and implementation to pay off, it is important that your marketing attract the right client. You want to attract your ideal client, and if you're not sure who your ideal client is, then you want to go back to strategy and research that further.

Consistency

Any marketing plan that is not consistently followed will not succeed. It is important that you strategize, implement and attract your target client on a consistent basis. This means writing blogs, content, and re-evaluating how that content is reaching out to and attracting clients.

SIMC is a complete approach in a four parts. Each individual part will not work when isolated on its own. By combining strategy, implementation, magnetism and consistency, you have a sure-fire strategy that will continue to attract your potential client over and over for years to come.

Cheryl Says:

Without a strategy, you're doomed from the start. Any smart business owner knows that a successful business is a direct result of planning. SIMC is a four part strategy with a complete approach. As you are reading this book, use the notes pages to keep track of your plans for Strategy, Implementation, Magnetism, and Consistency.

Why We Do What We Do

We do what we do to use what we know (and love) to make effective marketing on the Internet easier and more accessible for busy professionals. We do it to communicate our clients' messages with people through social media channels and to give a voice to their small businesses. We give our clients a competitive edge over their competition so that they can concentrate on providing outstanding service to their clients.

Success can only be manifested by helping others succeed. There are too many people on the Internet willing to take advantage of small legal professionals with quick fixes and false promises. We will only ever realize our success as a company by helping other businesses to their success.

Running a business shouldn't mean running around aimlessly with 'your head cut off'. Yet as business owners, we often feel like we spend a large part of the week just trying to 'catch up catching up'. Your clients pay you for your expertise. They leverage your knowledge. By leveraging the expertise of others, we can get more done in less time.

Most of our clients come to us after spending a lot of time, money, or both on Internet marketing that does not work. They know that something needs to change, but they are not sure what 'it' is. Often they have spent a lot of money on patches and 'quick fixes' that just aren't working.

We make effective marketing on the Internet easier and more accessible for busy professionals. By leveraging our expertise for your business, you can get back to providing the best service possible to your clients.

We are here to help you succeed! That's why we do "what we do".

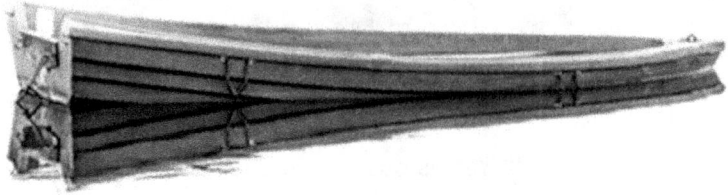

"Should you find yourself in a chronically leaking boat, energy devoted to changing vessels is likely to be a more productive than energy devoted to patching leaks."

— Warren Buffett

WHOM THIS BOOK IS FOR

As an alternative to our VIP done-for-you services, this book is for busy professionals looking to expand their marketing strategy and online presence. If you are trying to grow your business, but don't have the time to manage Internet marketing, and are frustrated by the inability to find a simple solution, then this book is for you. If you realize how important Internet marketing is to your business, but you're not sure how to apply it to your profession, then this book is for you.

Ultimately, this book is for the busy professional that opens their business only to find out that it is nearly impossible to run a business, market the business on the Internet, provide service to their clients, and still have time for a life outside of the business.

WHOM THIS BOOK IS NOT FOR

This book is not for those that are looking for a quick fix, cheap 'out', or a 'magic button'. It is also not for those that are looking to 'buy success' with zero effort on their part.

If you don't realize the importance of a consistent Internet marketing strategy or if you are looking for a cheap 'it will do' system, then this book is definitely not for you.

Lastly, this book is not for lazy people. Marketing takes work and costs you money – most times it will cost more of one or the other. You can hire someone to do the work for you or you can put your work boots on and dig in to the content in this book. On the road to success there is always choice. Not making a decision is also a choice. It is a choice to be lazy. If you are lazy, then this book is not for you.

"Opportunity is missed by most people because it is dressed in overalls and looks like work."

- Thomas Edison

WHAT WILL YOU LEARN FROM THIS BOOK?

In this book, you will learn how to attract more clients, dominate your local geographic area, and never ever have to worry about where your next client is coming from. My team and I compiled information on every area of marketing that we manage for our clients. I then took that information to create this book in a format that you can use to implement these strategies in your own business. We have a lot of information for you throughout this book, so take advantage of the end-of-chapter notes pages.

It is not my intention to have you implement every strategy in this book. It is also not my intention to explain every area of everything we do for every client. Each client has specific needs. We customize a strategy for each client as you must customize your strategy for your business. The pages in this book will provide you with authoritative information and allow you to develop a strong Internet marketing strategy that you must then implement to attract your target client.

So what are you going to learn? You are going to learn strategies about social media, content, traffic generation, competitive search engine optimization, blogging, articles, local Internet marketing, responsive website design, video marketing, and publicity advertising as they apply to the business owner.

Most importantly, you are going to learn how the smartest legal professionals crush their local competition and **how you can too.**

LET'S GET STARTED!

Now you know who we are, why we do what we do, whom this book is for, whom this book is not for, and what you will learn from this book.

So, let's get started!

"Stop selling. Start helping."

- Zig Ziglar

CHAPTER 1: CONTENT STRATEGY

Everything begins with content. In creating your strategy, content is the core component. Whether you are considering writing a blog post, an article, website content, or creating a video, you must first decide on the content. The content that you choose will depend on the target market or target client that you are trying to reach. Always keep in mind that specific person to whom you're talking. Much of your content may be for search engine optimization purposes, but you must always keep in mind that your target market will be reading or viewing your content. Write your content for that person. What would help your target client?

WHAT IS CONTENT STRATEGY?

Content Strategy is a concept that regards content development and marketing as a comprehensive, plannable process. Rather than viewing all components individually, content strategy creates a plan to market a business or product via content distributed throughout many media forms. Through a carefully considered content strategy, a business is able to effectively create and distribute their marketing content in the most effective and efficient way possible.

Being able to create consistently good content should be the cornerstone of your content strategy. Doing so can only result from detailed research, trend analysis, an active attunement to client needs, and ongoing concern for the what the future may hold within your specific market. In short, you must become a master student in a field of study that refuses to remain static. Figure out what is working for you, what is working for other people, and develop a strategy accordingly. You want your content to be visible on your website and on your social media accounts, and you want people to find and share it. Content strategy is complex and resistant to mastery by its very nature, but we can start by keeping 4 major goals in mind:

The 4 Primary Goals of Content Strategy

1. Create original, helpful, and informative content based on search trends and market research.

2. Establish an optimal rhythm of content creation, and track feedback and effectiveness so as to adjust your content strategy.

3. Make your content visible, sharable, and promotable via your website and social media. You want your content to top Google searches, and you want the people reading your content to promote it for free.

4. Track your content's effectiveness, and constantly rework your content strategy to reach wider audiences.

Remember that this is a holistic approach to maximizing your visibility and marketability, but it also fundamentally relies on an acute attention to detail. Your content strategy should be formulated with consideration to your business as a whole, as well as to each individual component. Success requires that you are able to figure out what people are searching for, what kinds of media they are coming into contact with, and how your business can stand out within this landscape.

An effective content strategy takes advantage of many media forms, both online and off. Each medium is subject to its own particular set of guidelines and standards. The major objectives of your content strategy may vary depending on the medium. Content tied to more palpable media forms may prove most effective for corporate communication, establishing credibility, building relationships, and cultivating loyalty. Online content can be effective in promoting product communication, boosting awareness, and converting viewers into clients. The key is to approach it from as many angles as possible, and to keep ahead of trends (or at least keep up with them).

Only by establishing and executing an effective content strategy, can you gain a leg-up on your competition. If a medium for communication exists, your competition is figuring out how to use it most effectively to gain visibility for their business. Clients will always pick the lowest hanging fruit. You want your content to be good, but if it's on the 5th page of a Google search, no one is going to see it. Your goal is to draw people to your website, your social media accounts, and your doors, and then for there be to be substance when they get there.

In short, your content strategy is a complex puzzle that must form an image when you put the pieces together. It is the difference between a large, loyal client base, and a waning profit margin. Stop looking at content as a necessary evil, and begin to examine it as an effective tool deserving strategy and consideration.

When you begin developing a content strategy for your business, start first with the completed image. What are you trying to achieve? Only then will you be able to figure out which shapes the pieces may take. Always keep in mind: this is no exact science. Flexibility is key. Roll with the punches, learn, and adapt. And remember, if the opposition is ahead, they must be doing something right. Figure out what it is and then create content around it.

What do I Write About?

People are looking for answers or solutions. They're really only interested in themselves. It's called WIIFM: What's in it for me? You need to solve common problems and answer questions that your potential clients have. If you don't have the time to write, use ghost writers, and then proof and approve their work. You can also have an assistant edit and approve ghost-written work, or even have an assistant write some of your content.

How To Develop A Content Marketing Strategy For Your Website And Blog

To develop a content marketing strategy for your website or blog you must first take a close look at your target market and decide what information is most important to them. If you do not know who your target market is, then take a look at your last four or five clients. How old are they? Are they married or single? Where do they live? What is their income? These are all important questions to answer in determining your content marketing strategy.

Remember that content is not limited to written content. Content can be comprised of images, video, display ads, and various other types of content. As you create your content for various marketing campaigns, you want to make sure that the content is going to appeal to your target market. There are various market research tools available on the web to help you better understand what "it is" that your target market is looking for when they come to your website or blog.

If you have a large number of clients or previous clients, then you can always create a survey and ask them directly. There are services like SurveyMonkey.com that will allow you to create and send custom surveys. This is a good tool for sending surveys to your own list of current and past clients.

Google also has some good marketing planning tools at thinkwithGoogle.com. One of these tools is Consumerbarometer.com. The consumer barometer tool helps you to discover how your target market uses the Internet. You can explore key findings from Google research or use their graph builder to build your own analyses based on the Google consumer that they have collected. Other tools on ThinkwithGoogle.com allow you to use real-time search data to dive into consumer search behaviors. There is also a specific research tool for YouTube that will allow you to compare training videos by age, gender, and location. If you're interested in analyzing the consumer's journey online and how it affects purchase decisions, you can use the Google tool called "the client journey to online purchase". All of these tools can help you gain better insight into how your target market is behaving online. This information can help you better craft your content to attract your target market in the most effective way possible.

How Do I Use a Blog?

Most clients don't know how to use a blog to attract new clients. They desire to reach an intended audience, but don't know where to start. A blog is basically a collection of articles about your opinions and advice on your area of expertise. It could be written as questions and answers and offer advice to potential new clients. You can write about common misperceptions in your field of expertise or insider tips, or tricks of the trade. You will want to personalize your blog and reach out to your target client. If you don't have time to write your own blog posts (which you shouldn't), consider hiring a professional company that will incorporate your personality into your blog posts.

Cheryl Says:

Attracting new clients on the Internet requires relationship building. Blogging is an important part of creating a relationship with a prospective client. Write about what you know. Start your blog with any frequently asked questions. When prospective clients comment on your blog, be sure to respond in a timely manner.

"Blogging is to writing what extreme sports are to athletics: more free-form, more accident-prone, less formal, more alive. It is, in many ways, writing out loud."

~Andrew Sullivan

CHAPTER 1 NOTES

What I Learned:

_____

_____

_____

_____

_____

_____

_____

_____

_____

_____

_____

Notes:

_____

_____

_____

_____

_____

_____

_____

_____

_____

_____

_____

_____

_____

_____

_____

_____

_____

_____

_____

_____

3 Things For Me To Implement From This Chapter:

_____

_____

_____

_____

_____

_____

_____

3 Tasks For Delegation:

_____

_____

_____

_____

_____

_____

1 Question For Cheryl:

_____

_____

_____

CHAPTER 2: BLOGGING STRATEGY

Blogging is a simple, effective way to create awareness for your website, and bring in potential clients. Regularity and consistency are key, and a planned blogging strategy is important to keep the process running continually over time. Effective blogging requires an understanding of what people are searching for and why, researching of relevant topics, writing helpful blog posts, and incorporating keywords into your posts strategically, but honestly.

Blogging is an area with which many businesses reach out for outside help. You can hire a professional writing company, use a freelancer, or write the blog posts yourself. If you must write your own blog articles, however, this chapter can help with the process of creating a blogging strategy to maintain better blogs, update them more consistently, and save time in the process.

Plan Your Blogs

A blogger is more than an online writer; they are a planner, a publisher, and an editor. Keep yourself ahead of the game, and your head above water, by setting a schedule to stay on track. Decide how many blogs you will be writing per month, and at what intervals you wish to publish them.

Since research is required to make blogging worthwhile, make sure to spend the time to plan the topics in advance. The key here is keeping track of trending search topics within your field. See where your business's website stands in relation to your competitors in certain areas, and use blogging to boost your visibility wherever needed. If you find that keeping up an effective blog takes too much time away from your business itself, enlist an Internet marketing company to help.

Blog Research

Every month there are thousands of blog articles posted online. To stand out amongst the crowd, you need to make sure that your blog posts are well-written and well-researched. Include facts and figures to add value to your blog. Enrich the blog further with keywords, which will ensure that your clients can find you easily by the topic of your blogs. Remember, you want your blog posts to be relevant to what people are searching for. The content has to match the title and be relevant to the topic.

Writing and Uploading your Blog Posts

First and foremost, you want your blog posts to do what they say they are going to do. Your blog posts should stay on topic, provide relevant and useful information, and positively represent your business. Make sure to edit your posts, and enrich them with search-engine-optimized keywords, relevant images, and links to your main website and social media accounts, before you upload each article to your blog.

SIMC provides full done-for-you management of your blogging, social media, search engine optimization, and website services. Learn more with FREE training for legal professionals provided at GoSIMC.com.

Blog Promotion

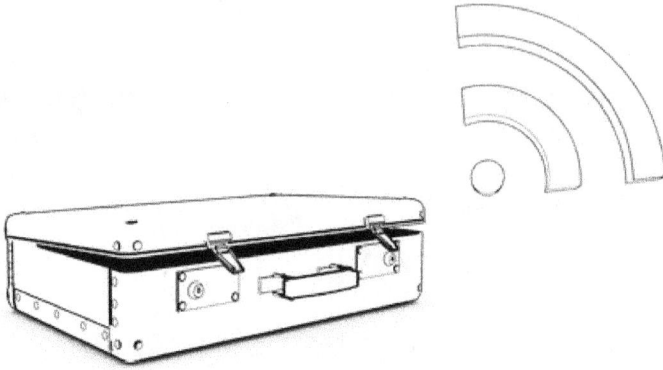

Once an article is completed and uploaded to your blog, the blogging process is not necessarily completed. You must still consider promotion. Some ideas for promoting you blog posts include:

- Tweet or post about your blog articles on other social media accounts to gain further attention and web traffic.

- Tie the content or keywords within each post to other posts, pages, or links on your website. Track and diversify content to reach wider audiences with each blog article.

- Send links to colleagues, well-known bloggers, and even regular readers, requesting their comments and feedback.

Track Blog Popularity with Analytics

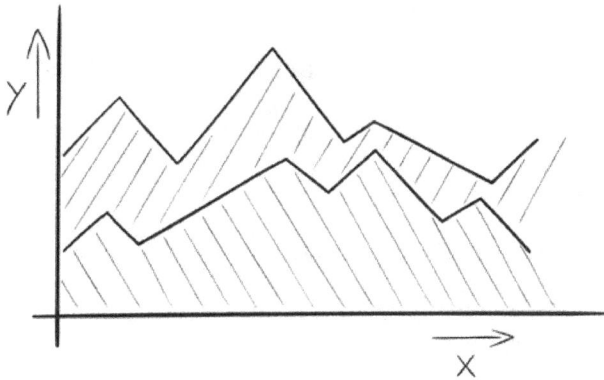

Always ask yourself this question: are your blog posts helping you achieve your goals? You want blogging to be an effective marketing strategy, not a waste of time. Track and measure the effectiveness of each post, and figure out what you can do to make them more effective. For example, using Google Analytics can help you track the traffic rate on your blog, or the number of conversions (new clients or newsletter subscribers). Keeping track of popular blog posts allows you to better plan your future blog articles. Understanding visitor behavior will also give you new ideas for blog articles that you may have not thought of otherwise.

How To Use Your Blog As A Traffic Magnet

Your blog has the potential to become a finely tuned machine, capable of driving consistent traffic to your website. This does not happen by chance or luck, but rather through the skilled crafting of a blog that contains all of the right elements. There are many small details that can make a tremendous difference in how visible your blog is, and how well it is perceived by your potential clients.

Use The Right Keywords to Reach your Target Audience

Figuring out the right keywords for your blog posts requires a high degree of self-knowledge. People search for a lot of different things online; you need to figure out what people are searching for that is relevant to your service offerings.

Consider who exactly your audience is and what message you want to get out to them. Once you understand what people are searching for, and how these searches properly relate to your business, craft your articles around these searches. Work backwards. Don't just write a post, and then try to shoehorn keywords in later. Remember, you're not smarter than Google; play by the rules.

Incorporating keywords that best describe your business will add relevance to your web content and increase your rankings in search engines, as the spiders will more easily be able to locate and index the pages on your blog. NEVER keyword stuff (use too many repeating or irrelevant keywords on the page) and do your best to create a natural flow throughout the blog. Understand that people use different phrases when searching for the same thing. Using the same phrase over and over is not only annoying, but it will also hurt your rankings in search engines.

Think about each specific service or product your company has, and then think about all the ways a person may search for that item. For example, if you are a personal injury attorney, then you will want to use keywords that are relevant to the different types of personal injury cases you would like to attract.

Be creative, and remember that your audience doesn't have the technical expertise that you do, and might not use the same language. Explain acronyms and spell out the full meaning of any industry terms in parenthesis. If you frustrate your reader or make them feel inferior, they will not read the rest of your article. Use the lowest grade level of communication for your target market. It is more important that they understand (and trust) you, then it is for you to use "big words" that are necessary to the subject of your blog post.

Research Other Blogs and Websites

Especially at first, it may be a good exercise to look through competitors' blogs, or blogs within a similar field. Type a keyword which you would like to use into Google, and see which blogs come up first. Read through the content, and get a feel for how a successful blog post might look. Get to understand how to incorporate keywords into the body of a blog post in a seamless way, which does not disrupt the flow or effectiveness of the writing.

Never Plagiarize

Always make sure to never plagiarize or copy content from another website. You want your content to be accurate and you want it to serve an important purpose, but you also want it to be 100 percent original.

Immediately Gain the Attention of
Your Potential Client

Create a title that is punchy, relevant, and gets the attention of potential visitors. If the title gives the reader an indication that the blog will provide them with information that is useful, they are more apt to keep reading. If you're having difficulty getting started (which is common) think about what would get your attention on a news stand and make you want to read the article.

Another tip for designing a great title is to think about your target audience. What are their genders, ages, preferences, etc. Think about what you would say to them if they were standing right in front of you, and you will have the beginnings of a great title.

The main purpose of your title is to get the reader to actually read your blog. So it is important that you spend time on the title. Think of your title as "click bait". If your title stood alone in a list, will somebody click on it? A useful tip is to look at the headlines for the National Enquirer and other sensational news publishers. Although you would not necessarily use those headlines, think how they grab your attention. These publications have been in business for many decades based on the efficient and effective use of **attention-getting headlines**. Another good place to look for ideas is in the back of these publications. In the classified section are many ads that cost quite a bit to the advertisers on a 'per word' basis. These ads are tested over and over again for effectiveness because of the cost. While, again, you would not use them word-for-word, you can use them for ideas on what is effective in getting people to respond.

Give Your Readers Reasons to Visit Your Blog

By presenting the reader with interesting and useful facts, and demonstrating how your blog will provide an answer to their questions, you are giving people a reason to engage with your blog, website, and your business.

Provide a preview of what your site has to offer. In doing so, you will build anticipation and excitement, while asserting authority and value. Only promise what the site can honestly deliver. Making claims that are not adequately supported can result in a loss of traffic and business. In many professions, it is also unethical and possibly illegal to misrepresent the truth about your business or services. It will also lead to a loss of trust which is the most damaging of all (besides getting arrested for fraud which would be a real buzz-kill for trust). If you lead the reader on to believe that they will find something on your site that isn't there, they will be disappointed, and will probably not visit your web site again.

Outline the benefits of your services without exaggeration, but with a definite promise of what the reader can gain by engaging further with your business. This will draw like-minded people to your blog to discover more of what you have to offer in your articles, and plant the seed for future clients or clients.

Distinguish Yourself from the Competition

If there is something that is unique to your business that you can offer better than your competition (and there should be if you are to be successful at all in competing against your competition) then make sure to stress that difference in all of your communication with your target market. Every blog is another opportunity to attract potential clients. Don't pass on the opportunity to tell them why you are different than any other option available to them.

Avoid the Use of Filler and Irrelevant Information

Your blog will be the most effective if you maintain a natural flow of well-written content. Yes, it is important to include the proper key words, but if there are keywords repeating over and over, then your message loses its authenticity and readability. Keep your wording concise and to the point. Avoid rambling or including information that does not add to your specific intended message.

If you find your descriptions becoming repetitive (especially when writing about topics such as law), use synonymous adjectives as much as possible. Repetition will make your blog come off as boring and uninspired.

Proof reading and revising for a natural, conversational flow can also help you greatly strengthen the content and readability of your blog. You want your content to be authoritative and professional, but you don't want it to read like a textbook. Read your blog posts aloud to see if they are easy to understand.

Build Content as a Reflection of Your Personality

People like to do business with people, not necessarily with businesses. Each business has a unique personality, and this in itself can serve as a magnet for web traffic. If your business does not currently have an online personality, then develop one. Use your own personality and let it shine through your communications with your target market. You have the ability to shape the feeling that your blog promotes with the content that you include in both your website and your blog. Your blog should reflect some important aspect of your site. It can be a how-to blog, a free informational blog, or the provision of tips that give your readers some further information regarding topics dealt with on the site itself, aimed to help them in some way.

It is here that you build interest and give your target audience a taste of what is to come by visiting your site. The pages of your website itself serve to promote your business and specifically describe the services which it offers. The purpose of your blog is to lure potential clients or clients in, provide them with useful free content, and then direct them to your main site. A blog post isn't a commercial for your business, but it can serve many of the same functions.

Insert High Quality Links That Reinforce the Content and Tone of Your Website

Links are a vital component in turning your blog into a traffic magnet for your main website. The concept is quite simple once you've had a little experience with it. Remember, each element of a blog post serves a particular role. Your title is designed to catch the attention of the reader with a strong hook that makes them curious. The initial lines of the blog further increase their interest by providing them with interesting facts or information that are useful in some way, while also relevant to the topic of your article.

The links provide your readers with a fast and easy way to access your main website. High quality links are those that are fully functional, and take the visitor directly to the part of your main website that relates to the promises or inferences which are made in the blog article.

Maintain Fresh and Exciting Content

Your blog needs to be updated regularly and consistently to include fresh and new information that gives your readers something new and exciting to explore. This also provides search engines with more information to index for your website. It builds relevance. It builds credibility. And, most importantly, it drives traffic to your website. As you build relevance and credibility, your blog will also consistently drive web traffic to your site from multiple search engines.

Branding and Consistency as a Traffic Magnet

Consistency in updating your content will help you to build your reputation and your brand. This will make your site stand out above the others because of its uniqueness and the wealth of content. The name of your site will remain in the memory of your target audience as a reliable and enjoyable resource of information on your topics. This will brand you as the go-to expert when your potential client has questions or is looking to hire the services of a professional.

When visitors return to your blog and your site, they will know that they can return later for fresh content. Nothing is worse than a blog that hasn't been updated for months or years. You should include a few lines near the end of the blog article that let the readers know who you are, and why they should listen to you. Always move your readers in the direction of your main site, but try to do it naturally and with tact.

Try not to become a person of success, but rather try to become a person of value.

~Albert Einstein

Engage Visitors and Allow Them to Get to Know You

Create links within your blog that allow visitors to follow your site on social media, and to interact with you and other readers. Invite them to share their opinions and leave their comments. This will help to further impress your brand in their memories, and it will also actively engage them in conversations about your blog and web site. Interaction of this type can stimulate a real and genuine interest in returning to your site and drive more traffic your way. All you need to do is say a few words about yourself and give an opinion that stimulates conversation. This allows your readers to connect with you on a more personal level, and to build their confidence in (and enjoyment of) your blog articles and main website.

Create a regular schedule to drop in and interact with viewers who begin conversations. This is an excellent and enjoyable way to drive traffic to your site, build your brand, and promote your message to an increasingly larger audience. If you don't have the time to engage with readers via your blog and social media, consider hiring someone to do it for you. Social media is a powerful way to reach your target market and it is definitely not to be ignored.

*SIMC can help you plan your blogging, social media, search engine optimization, and website strategies. Get your FREE copy of **Internet Marketing Makeover: Your 60 Day Strategic Marketing Blueprint with Step-by-Step Walk-Throughs to Crush Your Competition on the Internet** at SIMCcorp.com/makeover.*

Cheryl Says:

Social media interaction is about being social with your potential clients. Provide links to your social accounts to allow potential clients to interact with you on their preferred media platform. You should maintain a business presence on Google+, Twitter, Facebook, LinkedIn, and Pinterest and lead potential clients to your website and blog.

Connect with Cheryl

 +StrategicInternetMarketingCorpVeroBeach

 Twitter.com/strategicimcorp

 Facebook.com/strategicimcorp

 Linkedin.com/in/cherylwaller

 Pinterest.com/strategicimcorp

CHAPTER 2 NOTES

What I Learned:

_____

_____

_____

_____

_____

_____

_____

_____

_____

_____

_____

_____

_____

Notes:

_____

_____

_____

_____

_____

_____

_____

_____

_____

_____

_____

_____

_____

_____

_____

_____

_____

_____

_____

_____

3 Things For Me To Implement From This Chapter:

_____

_____

_____

_____

_____

_____

3 Tasks For Delegation:

_____

_____

_____

_____

_____

_____

1 Question For Cheryl:

_____

_____

_____

"Successful people ask better questions, and as a result, they get better answers."

~ Tony Robbins

CHAPTER 3: TRAFFIC GENERATION STRATEGY

The only way to gain new clients from the Internet is to generate traffic in the first place. Having a pretty website does nothing unless it is doing something to bring clients to your door. There are many ways to generate traffic. Search engine optimization is important to get your website indexed highly with different search engines. Articles and blogs help you to build relevance and credibility and attract others to link to the content on your website. Social media helps you to generate traffic by sharing useful and interesting information on different social media sites. Traffic can also be generated from off-line sources such as print and display advertising in newspapers and magazines.

Drive Traffic To Your Website With Time Tested And Amazingly Effective Strategies

The first question most professionals ask is; can I just buy traffic? A lot of people think that this is an easy answer. Why not just buy traffic and drive it to your website? Why not just pay a web service to push traffic directly to your website? The question is; can you? Of course you could. Should you? Absolutely not. What you're going to get if you try to buy traffic is a bunch of fake traffic in the form of Internet robots coming to your website. These robots are not going to convert into clients. This traffic is normally generated from spam pop-ups and pop-behind ads that people are not even aware of when they are visiting other websites. So, the traffic will never convert.

I am not talking about paid ads like Facebook ads or Google AdWords. I am referring to buying bulk traffic. Buying bad traffic will also increase your bounce rate. A bounce rate is a measurement of the percentage of people that both enter and leave your website from the same page. If the bounce rate increases, then you are effectively telling Google that people are not finding the information that they are looking for and they are immediately leaving your website. This is definitely not a strategy that you want to employ in your marketing. If you want to generate good leads and good traffic, then you need to concentrate on attracting that traffic to your website with good content.

You can generate good content in a variety of ways to drive traffic to your website. One of the most effective ways to build organic traffic is to provide content on your website and blog. Organic traffic is that traffic brought to your website without the use of paid ads or pay-per-Click advertising (PPC). You also want to do this on social networks and industry blogs. The most important part of this is to make sure you are posting good content. Because if you are paying someone to post content for you and it is not quality content, then there is no sense in posting anything at all.

You are generating traffic to your website by posting useful information that potential clients will want to engage with and comment on. You also want to use keywords and incorporate content around them to ensure that you're coming up in search engines for relevant searches. If your content is garbage, you will get garbage for traffic.

How Do I Track Website & Blog Visitors?

You want to make sure that you are using Google Analytics and Google Search Console (formerly known as Webmaster Tools). There are other tools besides Google Analytics and Google Search Console, however these are some of the best tools to use in analyzing your traffic. Google Analytics allows you to deeply analyze the traffic on your website. You can segment traffic and age, gender, interests, geographical location, behavior, or technology. You can take a deep look into how you are acquiring traffic with paid and organic efforts. If you are using Pay-Per-Click (PPC) through Google AdWords, then you can link your Google Analytics and Google AdWords accounts so that you can look deep into visitor behavior and optimize your campaigns. By linking your Search Console to your Analytics account, you can identify landing pages that have opportunities for higher search results.

If you notice in Google Analytics that a key phrase has an average positioning in search engine results, but has a really good click through rate, then people may have trouble finding these pages. You can increase your traffic to your website by helping people find these pages. The way that you help people find the pages is by optimizing the content on the pages. This can be as simple as adding additional content to existing content. You will want to have anywhere from 500 to 700 words on each page. So, if you come across a page that only has about

250 words on it, then you want to at least double the amount of content on that page. The more content you provide on a page, the easier it is for search engines to understand the information.

Another way to track how people find you is to use call tracking. Call tracking can be setup with all of your marketing efforts to keep track of your ROI (return on investment). With this type of tracking, you use a different telephone number for each media. All phone numbers ring your business phone number, but with the added benefit of knowing exactly where the lead came from. Yes, you can ask people where they heard about you. But, call tracking is much more reliable. Most people either don't remember or remember incorrectly. With call tracking, you always know exactly where the potential client found you.

Call tracking is especially important when you are spending money on print advertising. You want to make sure that every dollar you spend is bringing you clients. If you run an ad and it produces zero results, then stop running the ad or change it. DO NOT under any circumstances run the same ad over and over again hoping for different results. The print advertising company will tell you that it takes X number of times for their readers to see your ad before they will respond. This is not true. Your ad either works or it does not work. The only reason they need you to run your ad X number of times is to get additional revenue for their company; not for yours.

How Do I Increase Traffic

on My Website?

The easiest way to increase traffic on your website is to spend time analyzing the content on your site for opportunities to increase the traffic that it is currently attracting. A good place to start is to log into your Google Analytics and click in the left sidebar where it says acquisition. Under the **Acquisition** dropdown, there is an area for **Search Engine Optimization** and under search engine optimization there is a section for **Queries**.

Here you will find a list of keywords for which your site is currently showing in search engine results. If you want to increase traffic, then the best way to do so is a start working on these keywords immediately.

Take each keyword and turn it into a page on your website. You will want to name the page with the keyword, make the heading that same keyword, and then write content around the keyword. Keyword density is still a subject of debate. However, I have found that using the keyword once in the first paragraph, once in the body of the content, and once at the last paragraph gets great results in search engines. Again, you will want to make sure there's at least 500 to 700 words on the page and that the content provides information that is useful to the potential client. One of the worst things that you can do is create a page just for robots and exclude the fact that a real human will be reading it. What will happen is that someone will find your information on the Internet (provided that you do a good job of building the page) but when they get to your page they will realize that the content is horrible and will simply leave your website.

The process to generating traffic with your blog is similar to this. You'll want to name the blog post with the keywords in the title and heading of the blog. You'll want to make sure that there's at least 500 to 700 words on the blog post and that the content provides information that is useful to the reader. Next, you'll want to hyperlink the blog post to a relevant page on your website. The best way to do this is to hyperlink the keyword that you are targeting to the page on your website that targets that same keyword. This is why it's so important to set up your website first with all of the keywords that you intended to, and then consistently post new blog content that links to your website using the same keywords.

Pay-Per-Click (PPC) Advertising

You can also generate traffic to your website using paid means like Google AdWords, Facebook ads or Twitter ads. Each of these require different tactics and different understanding of how the target audience works. With Google AdWords, you are targeting traffic that is already in the research phase of the buying process. You'll need to target your ads specifically to attract those people that are looking for your services.

Pattern Interruption Marketing

With Facebook ads and Twitter ads, you are looking at a different type of marketing. The people that you are targeting are not in any phase of the buying process. Your marketing will be interrupting something else that they are doing. You are interrupting a pattern of behavior that is entirely different from the buying process. You have to design your marketing differently when it is a pattern interruption.

This type of marketing stems from neuro-linguistic programming and is very effective as a sales tactic. The problem with pattern interruption on Facebook and Twitter is that people are prone to ignore anything that is perceived as marketing or sales. If you are the sales person in the room, they are going to run from you.

Think about when you are at your favorite electronics store and the sales guy comes up to you. What is your initial reaction? Normally, if you are browsing, your reaction is to try to get away from him as fast as possible. So, if your marketing resembles a salesperson in any way on social media, it will usually fail.

Cheryl Says:

When you are putting together your marketing strategy for Facebook and Twitter, be sure that it is entertaining or informative in nature. Remember that you are interrupting something else that they are doing, so don't blatantly advertise unless you're using paid ads. Offer something interesting or funny to start off the relationship!

CHAPTER 3 NOTES

What I Learned:

_____

_____

_____

_____

_____

_____

_____

_____

_____

_____

_____

_____

_____

_____

3 Things For Me To Implement From This Chapter:

_____

_____

_____

_____

_____

_____

3 Tasks For Delegation:

_____

_____

_____

_____

_____

_____

1 Question For Cheryl:

_____

_____

_____

"The only place where success comes before work is in the dictionary."
~Vidal Sassoon

CHAPTER 4: COMPETITIVE SEARCH SEO STRATEGY

Creating a competitive search engine optimization (SEO) strategy is no easy task. People use many different words and phrases to search for your services and you have to determine which of those words are of most value to your business.

Not only do you have to decide which words are of most value, but you also have to determine the **order** of the words which are of *most* value. Then, once you determine the words in the "correct order" that are of most value to your business you have to individually decide how you are going to use those words on your website, your blog, articles, videos, and social media to attract the traffic and the potential clients that are already out there looking for you. Like I said, this is not an easy subject. I will go over basic tips in this section to help you optimize your own website.

Here Are 20 Useful Tips for Search Engine Optimization

1. **Commit to the time requirement**.

   Perhaps the most important step to take is to fully commit to the process itself on a long-term basis. You also will want to pay attention to the specific search engine optimization tactics that you use, because the ones you use this month or even the month before may not work the same way a second time.

2. **Plan your optimization.**

   There are four major things that all search engines look for: content, user experience, performance, and authority. Content is generally determined by the page's title, description, text, and overall theme. User experience comes into play when determining the look of the site, how easy it is to navigate through it, etc. Performance makes sure that your website works properly and quickly, while finally, the authority factor determines whether or not your website contains quality content. These are all things you will need to keep in mind when performing search engine optimization for your website.

3. **Have patience.**

It is important to remain patient during the process, as it can take approximately 3-6 months or more for organic results to take effect. This is especially true if you just started your site.

4. **Remain focused.**

Know what your overall business model is before moving forward with performing search engine optimization. There are some people who prefer not to take time to determine what their exact goals actually are, but in reality, it is extremely important that you do so and keep focused on these goals.

5. **Be willing to learn continuously.**

Become a search engine optimization student, especially if you are looking to do everything yourself. There are many informative resources that you can take advantage of, such as the Internet and many different books, in order to help you become successful in this.

6. **Analyze your efforts consistently.**

When you start everything, make sure that you have some form of web analytics put into place. It's important to have goal for all of your search engine optimization efforts, and web analytics software is an extremely important tool to have for that. This kind of software will help keep track of what's working and what isn't.

7. **Maintain current site maps.**

When constructing your website, be sure to include a separate "site map" page. This will help search engines find all of the pages on your site that are the most important, thereby increasing the chances that you will be found faster in search engine results. If your website is large, it helps to create multiple "site map" pages, ensuring that each one is kept within standards.

8. **Use accurate Metadata.**

Metadata is that data normally added to each web page by your web developer or search engine consultant. It tells search engines what the page is about and what to expect of the content on the page. A Meta title is simply the title of the page and the Meta description is the description that is provided to search engines. Place a Meta title and Meta description on your website that is both relevant and unique. In regards to search engine optimization, the title of the webpage is perhaps the most important factor. The Meta description, though it includes keywords, will not necessarily help your website get ranked in search engine results, but it will still appear underneath the listing in the results for some search engines. But, remember that not all search engines will use it.

9. **Do your research.**

When starting the project, do keyword research. This can be done by using one of the many available paid programs, as well as via free tools. Taking your time to select the correct keywords can save you countless hours of work. I recommend using Google Keyword Planner, WordTracker.com, or SEMrush.com for your initial research. Subsequent keyword research will be based on your traffic and future results.

10. **Pay attention to your URLs.**

Make each URL of your website search engine friendly. This can be done by using specific keywords for each of your pages within the URL. For example, a page about frequently asked questions would be named frequently-asked-questions in the URL (with dashes in between the words). A bad example is mywebsite.com/page-3.

11. **Use unique content.**

Create content that your users will find unique. For example, use a keyword tool to come up with your own service descriptions on each of your pages, as these keywords will be what searchers will actually be using on various search engines. Then, create content around those search phrases. Creating unique content is also a great way to obtain inbound links from other websites. When you share your content across communities, people will link to good content.

12. **Write for humans.** Write your page copy for humans first rather than for search engines. This is another area in which you should include different keywords that users are likely to use in searching for your site. However, you will want to make sure that you don't use a lot of unnecessary keywords, as this can get your page penalized. **NOTE:** Search engines are very advanced BS sifting machines. If you write BS, they will sift it out of the results. Write good content and concentrate on the potential client as a reader.

13. **Link internally with anchor text.**

When you begin internally linking your website (linking to pages on your website from other pages located on the same website), use your keywords as anchor text. This will help tell "Internet spiders" (which are programs that automatically fetch websites) what the page is all about.

14. **Write a press release.**

If you decide to publicity advertising, use it wisely. One of the best ways to gain more exposure for your website is by building relationships with all of the various media outlets in the specific area that you live in. If you choose to issue press releases online, this can not only effectively build links, but it can also bring you more exposure via multiple news websites.

*Visit **TheCelebrityMakers.com** for done-for-you publicity advertising that attracts media attention or call (866) 986-5650.*

15. **Use Webmaster tools.**

Many search engines will give you tools that you can take advantage of – <u>do it</u>. These tools will help you see exactly how many different search engines see your website, as well as include exactly how many inbound links that they're aware of. These tools include Google Search Console (formerly named Google Webmaster Tools) and Bing Webmaster Tools. Yahoo is part of the Bing Network, so using Bing Webmaster tools also applies to Yahoo.

16. **Diversify your traffic sources.**

Make sure that your traffic sources are as diversified as possible. Using search engines is always a good way to help drive traffic to your site, but other ways to do this can include newsletters and various other kinds of content that is subscriber-based. It will also help your business to create content via social media and blogs.

17. **Create a blog.**

Search engines index content from blogs more often than from websites, mainly because of all of the highly-structured data and constantly fresh content that they produce on a regular basis. Another useful tip involving this is to participate in other blogs so you can join in the conversation about the many different things going on in your industry. When commenting on other blogs, not only will you help drive more traffic to your website and increase your overall exposure, but you will also be able to obtain new links as well. Just be careful not to NEVER get involved in any link schemes. (Link schemes involve website owners liking to each other to improve ranking rather than to improve user experience.)

18. **Use social media wisely.**

Market on social media platforms as wisely as possible. For example, using photo-sharing websites such as Pinterest, Photobucket or Flickr is helpful if your business has a more visual-type element to it. No matter what size your business is, it's also helpful to use platforms such as Facebook and Twitter in order to post daily updates. Regardless of the social media platform you decide to use, it's important to keep in mind that you don't want to spam your page with loads of information. Always post relevant information in addition to your (limited) self-promotion.

19. **Use local search opportunities.**

By showing contact information such as your business's address, phone number, and detailed directions, you will be able to catch loads of local traffic looking for search terms that you have not yet incorporated into your website. It's also important to consider submitting your business's website to multiple business directories, where clients will be able to post reviews of your business. This can be done by listing your business information with the four major Internet data centers.

*Visit **GetMySnapshot.com** for an in-depth look what Internet data centers list for your business. The Free Snapshot report is a peek into what your business looks like online and how customers see you.*

20. **Network Your Business.** When building links, do so intelligently. While it may be easiest to start with a specific individual directory, you should instead focus on seeking out links from various authority websites that are in your particular industry. However, if offline networking is what you prefer, then take advantage of the services of such places as your local Chamber of Commerce and other local business networking.

"When you see a thing clearly in your mind, your creative "success mechanism" within you takes over and does the job much better than you could do it by conscious effort or "willpower"

~Maxwell Maltz

Maintain Correct Business Information With The Four Main Data Centers

There are four main data centers that provide information to hundreds of online directories, GPS, navigation, and business listing sites. These four main data centers are Neustar/Localeze, Factual, Acxiom, and InfoGroup. By maintaining a correct business listing on these four data centers, you save a lot of time in submitting your website to the smaller listing directories. These data centers do not push any information out, rather they maintain the lists that all of the smaller website directories pull from and maintain their information by comparing against these data centers.

We provide all of our clients this service and consistently keep their information updated, even if they move locations. If you would like to take care of your own listings, here are the links that you need to update your business listing with each of these data centers (some are fee-based):

acxiom.

mybusinesslistingmanager.myacxiom.com

factual.

www.factual.com/contact#update_add_business

neustar // Localeze.

www.neustarlocaleze.biz/small-business-services

infogroup®

http://www.expressupdate.com

Remember to check all four datacenters at **GetMySnapshot.com**

There are many other useful tips and suggestions that you can follow in order to successfully and properly perform search engine optimization for your website, but the aforementioned suggestions are definitely some of the basics that you will want to keep in mind. Search engine optimization is a long-term process and there are no viable shortcuts if you wish to have long-term success. If you are just starting out, these tips can help you get things moving until you are able to hire a professional. As your business grows, you will find that you have less time to dedicate to your website. While this is certainly good for your business, letting your search engine optimization get behind only allows your competition to gain the upper hand.

Some legal professionals will choose to hire an employee to handle search engine optimization, however professional services offer more quality than a single employee can provide at a lower cost than a full-time employee.

CHAPTER 4 NOTES

What I Learned:

_____

_____

_____

_____

_____

_____

_____

_____

_____

_____

_____

_____

3 Things For Me To Implement From This Chapter:

_____

_____

_____

_____

_____

_____

3 Tasks For Delegation:

_____

_____

_____

_____

_____

_____

1 Question For Cheryl:

_____

_____

_____

"You can't build a reputation on what you are going to do."

— Henry Ford

CHAPTER 5: WEBSITE DESIGN STRATEGY

Consider your website to be the online personification of your business and yourself. When it comes to Internet marketing, your website is the endgame. The goal of just about everything you do in your marketing is to drive traffic to your website and generate phone calls, but you don't want it to stop there. You need to convert the people who visit your website into clients.

Keep in mind that website design, SEO, and marketing are three separate functions. There are many times that we have had a client come to us with a website that was designed by someone they knew or a family member. This person did not necessarily mean to do any harm, but the website lacks certain elements that allow it to become properly indexed on the Internet and consequently convert clients. Sometimes our clients come to us having paid thousands of dollars for websites that do nothing more but look pretty. It is very rare that you will find an individual who is familiar with website design, search engine optimization, and marketing. So, the website falls flat on one or more areas. Sometimes you will find an individual that is familiar with one or two of these, but very rarely will you ever find someone who is familiar with all three. It is important that your website is not only designed well, but it must be search engine optimized to attract your target market in a way that will convert them into clients. Otherwise, you have nothing more than a pretty website that does nothing to bring new clients to your business.

You want your website to be the doorway into a relationship with potential clients. Once you attract people to your website, you want them to be able to email you, call you, or come to your office – whatever it takes for them to drop their online anonymity, and start engaging with you. For this to happen, your website needs to be professional, authoritative, and filled with calls to action and contact information to put the ball in motion.

Organization of Content

The need for professional designers and the size of the design team will be determined by the level of complexity of the website. A Web-design team must be aware of your vision. They can also provide their insights from their experience on technical aspects. Before the actual coding, content must be organized into pages that will be linked in the navigation menu.

A first impression is always the lasting impression, so the landing page must look good regardless of how much content that goes in it. With modern search engines, that first impression could be from any one page on your website. So, you must make sure that the entire website looks good, functions well, and encourages potential clients to contact you in one form or another.

Aesthetics and Design Standards

With all research and organizational goals in place, it is now time to make your choices of color, contrast, picture, typeface, font and the flow. Much work at this stage is allocated to the designers who will have to compute technical requirements, server capabilities and security protocols.

Note: Do not use FLASH for your website. Though it provides great interactive features, it reduces performance on slow connections and prevents full indexing of the content on your website. Responsive design, with HTML and CSS, creates some of the best looking sites with top performance across all browsers and devices.

Monitoring Traffic and Using Analytics

With the website launched and promoted, it is now time to monitor the performance. Tools like Google Analytics provide a user friendly interface to track site performance using graphical statistics. If all goes well, the site performs well with rapidly increasing traffic and maximized profits. If the site underperforms, then it's time to re-think strategies.

In the beginning, the most important part is to remember to add Google Analytics code to the website so that the statistics can be tracked and analyzed at a later date. At first, the website data will be hard to interpret because there is not enough content. But, after time has passed and content is added you will be able to start analyzing your data and find both issues and opportunities on your website.

How To Use Website Design To Make It Easier For Humans (And Robots) To Find The Legal Information They Want

Website development, search engine optimization, and marketing are all important components for your website. These must be considered separately and applied to your overall website strategy.

Website Development

The purpose of website design is to make the website easy to navigate and attractive to visitors. It must also be easy for search engines to index. Designing a website that displays quickly and provides a user-friendly experience is of utmost importance for human visitors as well as search engine robots. One of the many signals that Google uses to determine your search engine ranking is the speed at which your pages load and how easy the website is to navigate. If your website is using a lot of flash or large images that are difficult to load, then the page will load very slowly and possibly even timeout (not load at all). If Google is unable to load your page, then your page will never even be indexed by Google. This is very similar with other search engines, so it is very important to consider when designing your website.

Search Engine Optimization

There is a lot of mystery surrounding search engine optimization (SEO). It is simply a process that makes the website easier for search engines to index. This process uses Metadata that is located in the head of the page. This Metadata must be consistent with the content of the page. The Metadata in the head of the page is not something that a user will see nor will you necessarily know what information is there unless you are specifically looking for it. The three most important Metatags in Metadata are the Meta-title, Meta-description, and Meta-keywords. The Meta-title is used by all search engines when indexing the website. It is important that this Meta-title match the URL of the webpage, the H1 (main heading) title of the webpage, and the content on the page. The Meta-description is used by many search engines. Google does not necessarily use the description in their search engine results, however they do look at it to see how it compares with the content on the page. Meta-keywords is no longer used by Google at all, but it is considered by other search engines. It is best to use all three of these Meta-tags when search engine optimizing your webpages.

You can Google "How Search Works" and click on the first result in Google for a great explanation from Google on how search engines work. There really is no mystery at all to search engine optimization.

Google offers webmaster guidelines that spell out the do's and don'ts of optimizing your website for search. According to Google, some of these are: Use at least one text link for each page on your website, have a site map, be reasonable with the number of links on any one page, provide useful content, use words that users would use in a search, use text as links (not images), use Metadata and ALT links for images, check for broken links, write your content for users (not search engines), don't try to deceive the user or search engines. Some things that Google recommends that you do NOT do are: don't use auto-generated content, don't use link schemes, avoid duplicate content on multiple pages, don't use hidden links or hidden text, avoid the use of irrelevant keywords. In sum, use quality content and don't try to trick search engines. Avoid anything shady or not genuine in nature.

Cheryl Says:

An important fact to consider is that search engine optimization does not stop at the first page of your website. Each and every page of your website has a separate opportunity to rank highly for the specific key phrases on the website. The more you optimize your website, the more likely you are to show up on the first page of results for many terms.

What Can I Do on My Legal Website to Improve Search Engine Optimization?

Some of the things that can be done on your website are a little technical and are best left to your webmaster. If you're someone who likes to do things themselves, you can start by paying attention to the Metadata on your website. The Metadata on your website tells search engines what the page is supposed to be about and provides a bit of a description to robots that index your website. When you create the URLs for your website, be sure to use plain language and match the URL to the heading of the website. For example, if you were writing a website page on legal remedies in ABC County, then you would want the URL to be "legal-remedy-ABC-county", and your heading to be "Legal Remedy in ABC County". Then you would want your content to match the heading and the URL so that everything is uniform and that when search engines come through, they see that the Metadata matches the URL, matches the heading, and matches the content on the page.

Internet Marketing With

Call-to-Action

Now that you have your website developed and you have worked on your search engine optimization, it is time to look at your marketing strategy for the website. Every page on your website should have a call-to-action. A call-to-action instructs the visitor to take a particular action or to do "something". For example, some pages on your website may request that the potential client call your office. Other calls-to-action may include filling out a form or signing up for a newsletter.

You must look at each page individually and decide what the specific call-to-action will be for that page and make sure it is included on the page. The best place to place your call action is at the end of the content of the page. Even if the call-to-action is to have them go to another page on your website, you must tell them to do "something" or website visitors will do nothing at all.

The best call-to-action you can use is to have visitors request a book. Writing a book on your particular area of expertise sets you apart from your competition. It makes you an authority and creates interest where there was once resistance. A website visitor may not be interested in signing up for your newsletter or giving you his email address, but he might be very interested in requesting a free copy of your book.

*Writing a book is a very effective marketing tool and if you are interested in becoming an author of your own book, then visit **SIMCpublishing.com** or contact your team at SIMC Corp (866) 986 - 5650. We can help you write a short book (in much less time than you might think) or refer you to a specialist company that we work with to help clients write longer books.*

This is a matter of time or money. You are losing much of both without a book.

CHAPTER 5 NOTES

What I Learned:

_____

_____

_____

_____

_____

_____

_____

_____

_____

_____

_____

_____

_____

3 Things For Me To Implement From This Chapter:

_____

_____

_____

_____

_____

_____

_____

3 Tasks For Delegation:

_____

_____

_____

_____

_____

_____

1 Question For Cheryl:

_____

_____

_____

"The problem is never how to get new,

innovative thoughts into your mind, but how

to get the old ones out."

– Dee Hock

CHAPTER 6: RESPONSIVE WEB DESIGN STRATEGY

Responsive website design is a necessity for businesses that are serious about driving traffic to their websites. Over the past decade, the use of smart phones, tablets, and other mobile devices, has changed the way that people view websites. It has also changed the way that they use the Internet. The modern convenience of responsive design allows for faster browsing in any location and on any device. The benefit is that businesses have the opportunity to attract more visitors. The challenge is that, as a business owner, you must optimize your website for a variety of different devices. This is done easily with the implementation of a responsive website that automatically adjusts to the device of the viewer.

The Origins of Responsive Design

Responsive web design was first coined as a term by Ethan Marcotte in 2010. While not a new idea, it was an expansion of the technology that creates a fluid and flexible design that can be adaptable to any visual display device. The grid layout is designed to accommodate a wide variety of screen sizes used by those visiting the sites. It promised solutions that would be more easily adapted for future technology in Internet-enabled communications devices. An example is the need for retina friendly sites that are responsive to HiDPI displays such as HD televisions and MacBook Pros. These devices are used in a small percentage of current browsing, but this type of technology will evolve to become more prolific in Internet browsing.

NOTE: Retina friendly refers to devices that display images at a resolution that is nearly equivalent to print quality.

Why Responsive Website Design Works so Well

When shoppers browse Internet sites, they use a variety of different devices. Desktops and laptop computers were the main resources used just a few years ago. More recently, advanced technology has made it possible to surf the Internet via smaller hand-held devices such as tablets, smartphones, and other Internet-enabled devices. The website that has not been optimized for devices with smaller viewing screens may be difficult to access for many users. The images do not display properly, in most cases, and viewers become quickly frustrated. They then quickly move on to a site that they can more easily used on their device. A lack of responsive design decreases the number of viewers who may have otherwise converted into loyal clients (with future repeat business).

What Responsive Design Does for Your Website

This advanced technology optimizes your site so the content can be properly displayed on any type of device. The images come through quickly, clearly, and the size will be automatically adjusted for the device used. The links and features are made more accessible with fast download times. The sizing of images and text is one of the trickiest parts for optimization. What will load quickly and easily on a laptop may not fare as well on a smartphone. In addition to the current challenges facing website managers, finding a responsive design plan that will accommodate future technology is a consideration.

A single website design that is easily viewable from a variety of devices is preferred by Google and other search engines as it cuts down on the indexing of duplicate content. Responsive design is preferred by many, over designing one website for viewing on desktop devices and a separate website for mobile devices. Your search engine rankings will be higher with a responsive site (on mobile devices) and it will drive more traffic from a variety of devices. Using a desktop and mobile version is also twice the work and maintenance of a responsive design site. The use of responsive design also eliminates the common issues of redirects that are not fully functional and other navigation errors that frequently occur when switching from mobile versions to desktop versions. These websites are specifically designed for highly functional use from any type of Internet-enabled device.

How to Tell If Your Website Is Mobile Ready

The test for this is very simple. Pull out your smartphone and try to access your website. View the images and try browsing around. Are all of the images loading quickly? Can you read the important text? If you have any difficulties accessing or navigating through your site, so will your viewers. Users who become frustrated will go to your competitor's website and are not likely to return to yours. If your website does not display correctly on all devices then you need to upgrade to a responsive design. Google also has a mobile-friendly test that you can use to test your website and make sure that it has a mobile-friendly design. You can also get additional information for making a website mobile friendly from Google developers.

▶   *www.google.com/webmasters/tools/mobile-friendly/*

▶   *developers.google.com/webmasters/mobile-sites/get-started*

Cross Browser Testing

While you are testing your website for mobile compatibility, you should also check your website for browser compatibility. There many different browsers including Safari, Chrome, Internet Explorer, Android, Mac, iPhone Opera, and many more that you have probably never even heard about. It should never matter which browser your potential client is using, your website should look good and display well. You can test your website for free on crossbrowsertesting.com.

What You Can Do to Make Your Website More Responsive and User-Friendly

1) Avoid using plugins such as Quicktime, Flash or others that are not compatible for most mobile users. These components are notorious for slowing down the downloading process anyway.

2) On non-responsive sites , keep the header images 960px in width to avoid the need for excessive scrolling to see the image fully or correctly displayed. Fonts under 11px will be too small for a mobile user to read so keep fonts above this size. While mobile sites are inexpensive to create and can be customized specifically for access by smaller devices, they create the need to maintain and update a second website.

3) A better solution is to go with a responsive site that uses the same HTML code for all visitors, but has a built in mechanism for adjusting the display in response to the particular type of device that is used for access. The cost may be a little higher initially, but in the long run, the benefits will end up saving you time and money.

Considerations When Implementing Responsive Design

In order to implement a highly functional and responsive website design, you must ensure that the site is fully search engine optimized. Sites that are not, may experience slower downloading times and this would defeat the purpose of the upgrade. With proper optimization, your responsive website is the most efficient way to attract new clients using a variety of media devices.

Key Benefits of Responsive Website Design

Companies which have implemented responsive design websites are reaping the benefits and have a competitive edge over those who have not. Increased conversion rates are noted in many case studies as a result of this type of optimization. The factors which come into play in producing this higher conversion are increased search engine rankings with clearer mapping paths related to targeting shoppers and a higher client satisfaction rate with website ease of use. Users may access your site with a desktop one day and use a different device on another day. They expect the same experience regardless of the type of device they use to access your website. Consumers are looking for a smooth and efficient shopping experience. Consistency across media devices is a means of ensuring that your visitors are getting what they expect from your site and it encourages their repeat business.

Responsive sites with high quality content generally have lower bounce rates. (Remember, earlier I mentioned that a bounce rate is the percentage of visitors who enter and leave your website from the same page). It's a way to quantify the number of visitors not finding what they intended to find on their first visit.

Frustration is the main reason that visitors abruptly leave and this is usually because they cannot access the website properly (non-responsive design) or did not find the information that they were seeking. If a consumer has to spend time enlarging or scrolling through the images and links on your site to find what they need, they tend to leave and go to a site that is more user-friendly.

Increased Page Ranking in SERPs

Increased page ranking is another key benefit of responsive sites. SERPs stands for Search Engine Results Pages and are the pages that you see after you type in a search and click enter on Google, Yahoo, or Bing. Because the content of the site is easier to access and to index when it is created with responsive design, it is likely to be placed much higher in search engine results.

Cheryl Says:

A search engine's aim is to quickly provide users with sites that provide the content that they seek in terms of relevance and functionality. To rank higher in search engines, it just makes sense to provide a website that is easy to navigate and provides the information visitors seek. In the long run, a site built in responsive design is more time and cost efficient.

Sites that are divided between mobile and traditional formats may lose something in the design transition that relates to the users recognition and familiarity with the site. Consistency and uniformity are factors that influence a visitor's decision to do business with you.

Responsive websites may be initially more expensive to build, but as time goes by, they are more cost effective and do have the potential to yield much higher return on investment. There is decreased time and effort required for site maintenance and upgrades. Your company is likely to make up any cost differences merely by the increased traffic that is driven to your site.

Planning Future Internet Marketing for Your Company

Every day, it becomes more essential that your website provides convenient and user-friendly access for a variety of Internet enabled devices. It has become **more** than essential; it has become consumer expectation. Legal professionals employing websites that are not easily viewable from different devices will quickly lose clients to those attorneys that meet consumer expectation of multi-device compatibility.

The 'Mobilegeddon' Update

On April 21, 2015 Google released what many have called the 'Mobilegeddon' update. Although there was much speculation that the update would affect searches from tablets and desktops, Google has publicly announced that the update only affected searches for mobile devices.

The update continues to affect pages individually. If some pages on your website are not mobile friendly, it will not affect the ones that are mobile friendly. So, if you have 10 webpages that are mobile friendly and 20 pages that are not mobile friendly, the first 10 pages will show up in mobile searches while the other 20 may not. You can check individual pages by using the mobile friendly test provided by Google or by using the mobile usability report in Google Search Console (formerly Google Webmaster Tools). Either way it is important that you make sure that each of your pages are mobile friendly or they will not show up well in mobile searches. Google has confirmed that these pages may still show up in mobile results. They will just not have favorable ranking on mobile devices in comparison to mobile friendly websites.

Linking to non-mobile-friendly webpages from a mobile-friendly webpage will not affect that particular page's ranking. So, the most important thing is to make sure that each of the pages on your website is considered by Google to be mobile-friendly.

What Website Design Means to the Smart Legal Professional

The Internet is quickly becoming the best format for conducting business. As times change, legal professionals must be willing to adapt to the requirements for successful marketing and client service. Advances in technology have made it possible to keep up with consumer demands and responsive website design is an effective use of this innovation to maintain a competitive marketing edge. Although there are other ways to provide access for mobile device users, they have distinct weaknesses and disadvantages.

In addition to redundancy, creating dual sites (one for desktop and one for mobile devices) has a tendency to lower the overall perception of unity and can lead to lost conversions and lower search engine rankings. A customer that visits the desktop version of your website may not recognize the mobile version and vice versa. It is best to have just one version of your website. Smart legal professionals of tomorrow's businesses understand the long-term payoff and will employ responsive design in all Internet marketing efforts regardless of initial upfront cost.

Go with a Web Developer That Can Provide You with a Responsive Website

You can locate freelance website developers to professionally develop a responsive website design. This is the easiest way to go about making your website fully responsive. There are costs involved in this option, but in the long run, they will pay out in increased web traffic and conversion rates. You should always avoid trying to build your own website or make changes to your website. Even developers know that the smallest mistake could cause catastrophic failure of your website. Although it has already been pointed out, remember that website development is separate from search engine optimization marketing. If you hire a freelance website developer that is not familiar with search engine optimization or marketing, you could wind up with a pretty website that does nothing for you.

DO NOT BUILD YOUR OWN WEBSITE

My best advice to you on website design is to not attempt to create your own website. Although there are many tools out there that allow you to build your own website for free or at a low cost, most are templates that are duplicated hundreds of times on the Internet. What's worse is that many of these have the same exact content across the many different websites of the unsuspecting legal professionals that purchase the templates. So, if you're not aware of it and you use one of these websites, you're simply making your website irrelevant in the eyes of Google and other search engines.

It is always best to hire professionals to build your website and write quality content. You wouldn't hire your plumber to remove an aching tooth. You also wouldn't hire your accountant to repair your vehicle. So, then why would you hire yourself to build your own website? It just doesn't make sense. If you want a professional looking website that also indexes well in the search engines while marketing to your target market, hire a company that has experience in responsive website design, search engine optimization, and marketing.

💡 **Professional website design**, **search engine optimization**, and **marketing** are all extremely important to the success of your online marketing strategy.

Never settle for a company that provides only one or two of these and absolutely never settle for a company who tries to convince you that you do not need all three.

If you're interested in having a professional website designed with search engine optimization and Internet marketing as a complete package, then please contact your VIP team at SIMC Corp (866) 986 – 5650 or visit **SIMCcorp.com**.

CHAPTER 6 NOTES

What I Learned:

_____

_____

_____

_____

_____

_____

_____

_____

_____

_____

_____

_____

_____

3 Things For Me To Implement From This Chapter:

_____

_____

_____

_____

_____

_____

3 Tasks For Delegation:

_____

_____

_____

_____

_____

_____

1 Question For Cheryl:

_____

_____

_____

CHAPTER 7: LOCAL INTERNET MARKETING

With growing options in the Internet marketing realm, small businesses can now enjoy the level of exposure similar to that of a big brand, but within your local area. Branding your company can be as simple as maintaining consistency in all of your marketing efforts. Marketing your business on the Internet locally is as simple as talking about the local area in your articles, blogs, and on your website. The content you create on your website should refer to your local area as much as possible. Incorporating locality specific keywords and phrases in your SEO strategy is also extremely important. Above all, make sure that your business information and location is listed correctly with the four main Internet datacenters. If you have not done so already, go to **GetMySnapshot.com** and begin the process.

Local Attorney Branding

Local attorney branding is an often overlooked aspect. Branding is not just about spending big stacks of money for advertisement or star-studded promotions; it is about incorporating the theme of a business and presenting it visually to build an identity. The colors and elements of a logo visually present those ideas and also aid the designing process of a website and physical space. Branding makes websites stand out in the search results and attracts leads. You should spend some time strategizing the brand that is you. Incorporate your personality into your branding and create a brand that is unmistakably "you". Remember that people like to do business with people that they like, so become that person. Do not hide behind a logo or try to make yourself look like a big corporation. Most people would rather do business with a small firm because of the ability to build a closer relationship. Corporations are known to be cold and faceless entities. Don't be that.

Cheryl Says:

Let people know if you contribute time to the community or volunteer in any way. Share your story and let people know why it is that you do business in your local community. If you attend events or donate to local charities, then don't be afraid to let people know that on your website. Show that you are member of the community.

How Much Does It Cost To Market Locally?

Cost is entirely up to your budget and depends on what media you choose for marketing. Remember that it is important to target publications and media that your target market reads or watches. It's not about the publications, it's about the target market. There are many opportunities for what is called "out of place" marketing. For example, if your target market likes to play video games and subscribes to a certain videogame magazine, then it may be prudent to place an ad in that magazine. While other professionals are only placing their ads in what is "expected", you are gaining new clients from places that they may not expect you to be. But, because you are present in their favorite magazine, you are not competing against any of your direct competitors for the attention of that reader. It is considered out of place because one would not expect to find your advertising there, but it is a good way to reach your target market without the distraction of competing offers.

One of the most effective ways to target your local area in the search engines is to include information about your local area. An attorney might want to target keywords and phrases that include the name of the town or county. You might also want to consider target keywords and phrases that include the names of affluent neighborhoods and communities. Your articles should target the target client, the key legal remedy, and the geographical area that you service.

The more content you provide for potential clients and search engines, the better.

Search engines index content and are programmed to return the most relevant results for a user's search phrase. When a user is looking for your services, he or she will often times use the name of the area in their search phrase. This is becoming more and more common with the use of mobile devices. For example, a couple looking for a bankruptcy lawyer in a certain area may do a mobile search for attorneys with experience in chapter 13 or chapter 7 bankruptcies. Let's say for example that you have just written a blog about chapter 7 bankruptcies and you talked about how they may be able to keep their home depending on certain qualifiers. You may also have talked about how the bankruptcy laws allow for certain exemptions that may include the ability to retain certain personal property, like a car. Now when this couple does a search for keeping their home and car in a chapter 7 bankruptcy, guess who's coming up first? You are. Most attorneys are trying to target "my area bankruptcy attorney" while you are writing about different laws and what those laws may mean in context. The more you write about your profession, the more you will show for those results. Targeting your local area is as simple as *talking* about your local area and creating content that potential clients will find *useful*.

Cash In On Your Local Internet Marketing Strategy

The most important thing to keep in mind with local Internet marketing is that you should list your business name, business address, and business phone number on each and every page of your website. As search engines are indexing each page of your website, they associate that website with the geographical location you provided the search engine.

You should also make sure that you list your website with Google, Bing, and Yahoo maps. Each search engine has their own version of maps and it is a very good idea to submit your business information to them.

CHAPTER 7 NOTES

What I Learned:

_____

_____

_____

_____

_____

_____

_____

_____

_____

_____

_____

_____

3 Things For Me To Implement From This Chapter:

_____

_____

_____

_____

_____

_____

_____

3 Tasks For Delegation:

_____

_____

_____

_____

_____

_____

_____

1 Question For Cheryl:

_____

_____

_____

"Nothing great was ever achieved

without enthusiasm."

~ Ralph Waldo Emerson

CHAPTER 8: VIDEO MARKETING STRATEGY

Video, with its wide range of powerful narrative structures, is without-a-doubt an important medium for content creation. A video with a compelling story empowers clients to relate to your brand and to your story for the basis of a long-lasting relationship of trust and support. The concept of video marketing is misunderstood by those relatively new to the arenas. The point is not just to aim for the million-view milestones. Videos are an opportunity to form a relationship with a potential client before ever meeting the client. It leverages your time in introducing yourself and allowing clients to get to know you and why you do 'what it is' that you do.

Determine the Purpose of the Video

B2C (Business-to-Consumer) and B2B (Business-To-Business) video marketing are both a bit different. B2C marketing can focus on producing stylish videos like off-road SUVs bouncing on the dirt tracks. They work to seek out the type of viewership within the masses who would like to own a particular vehicle. That same approach may not work for B2B, which relies on producing minimalist videos about internal culture, individual stories, and project portfolios. Determining the purpose of the videos will also determine the targets for the campaign around which a strategy can be constructed.

Cheryl Says:

Concentrate on creating videos that allow your potential clients to get to know you and understand why you became the professional that you are today. Don't make the mistake of trying to hide behind your logo or corporate name. People want to do business with people, and they will much rather come to you as a person than as an entity.

Create short videos on different topics and discuss frequently asked questions or common client concerns. Your videos should be no longer than two to six minutes in length. Research has shown that most viewers will drop off around the two-minute mark. So, for the most part, keep your videos under two minutes if you can. If you're not sure how to create videos or are not computer savvy, then you can use a service like animoto.com to make professional looking videos with minimal effort.

► Animoto.com

Avoid scraping images from the Internet or "borrowing" images from Google image search. You can use services like dreamstime.com to purchase royalty-free images at an affordable price. Many images can be downloaded for as little as a dollar each depending on the package you purchase.

► Dreamstime.com

Video Production

The digital revolution has opened up the video industry to a lot of possibilities. Yet, much depends on who is hired for the job, whether it's a highly sought-after freelancer or an in-house producer. Creativity goes a long way in the process of content creation. If a brand implies a message that is difficult to communicate in live-action, then a highly imaginative team of expert animators will certainly be able to pull it off. When it is not possible to hire a professional production service, a HD

Camcorder on your shelf may be the option for the price of a little compromise.

Video 'Content' Marketing & SEO

Remember that video marketing is more than just about milestone hits or views. Most of the videos on YouTube fail to Influence viewers even with top production standards. It happens because the descriptions lack keywords or hyperlinked terms and go unnoticed by the search engines.

When uploading your videos to YouTube and other video distribution sites, make sure you always have the website address and your phone number in the description. The ideal place for your website address is before the very first word of the description. Always include a call-to-action in the description of your video and only include one call-to-action. You want to make it as simple as possible for people to respond or take the action that you want them to take.

Remember to use your keywords and phrases in the descriptions in the titles of all of your videos. You want to make it look natural and don't try to stuff keywords where they don't make sense. Remember that keywords inside the videos are not currently tracked by YouTube or

Google, but as technology improves this may not be far in the future. In the meantime, remember to type your keywords and phrases into the title and descriptions of all of your videos. If you can make a video for each and every keyword or phrase and make it to a particular page on your website, then this will go a long way to helping you with your overall search engine optimization strategy.

Marketing Channels and Tools

There are many video hosting channels on the web, for example, YouTube, Dailymotion, and Vimeo. It is good practice to increase your SEO performance by embedding videos from these channels into primary websites. It often converts leads into buy-ins and adds a premium appearance to the site.

Videos That Drive Mass Traffic To Your Site

Social media sites provide an excellent means of advertising your business to people who are the most apt to be interested in your content. This is quickly becoming one of the more popular tools that web marketers use to catch the attention of viewers and drive traffic to their websites. The beauty of video advertising is that you can not only tell people about your business, you can also show them at the same time. While you are promoting your site, you can also include elements in the video that result in increased search engine optimization at the same time. As with any marketing strategy, it must be done properly in order to be effective.

Write the Script to Appeal to Your Ideal Target Client

Consider who you are targeting in your video and what is most likely to catch their attention. The video content must reflect the theme of your business with regard to how legal services can provide solutions that will improve the viewers' lives. Who are the people who are most apt to benefit from the services? What is the best way to reach them? Consider the demographic, cultural, and emotional factors to write the script in a way that both tells the viewer about the discomfort of their issue. Then, provide a solution with benefits in the form of using your legal expertise to their advantage.

Always appeal to the values and emotions of your viewers. Give them a sound reason to visit your site for more information. The environment, setting, and tone of the video should be designed to evoke emotions and this is easily done by using props and elements that may be nostalgic or pertinent to your targeted group. You want to appeal to their emotions of how they will feel both before and after use of your services.

HOW TO SEARCH ENGINE OPTIMIZE YOUR VIDEO

Pay close attention to the title that you choose. The words and word combinations must be optimized to maximize the quality for search engine ranking and for catching viewer attention at the same time. The goal of the video is to take a multifaceted approach to search engine optimization for your site and get your content indexed by search engines for maximum rankings.

Keywords are descriptors that are used to alert search engine indexing robots to the appropriate classifications for your site. Remember that search engine indexing robots are your friend. They will index your website anyway that you ask them to, as long as you do it correctly. In order to drive the right type of traffic to your site, your video and the descriptions that you provide must include words that most closely describe the content. This includes words that relate to not only the services themselves, but additionally, that describe aspects of their uses.

Employ Long-Tail Keyword Variations for Pages

Statistics show that up to 90 percent of the traffic generated to websites occurs as a result of using long-tail descriptive tags. The long-tail keywords make it easier for spiders to index your site and increase your rankings in search engine results. They also are proven to result in higher conversion rates from website viewer to client. Understanding these facts gives you more tools in your video marketing arsenal.

Use Long-Tail Keywords

Cheryl Says:

People using queries in their searches usually look very specifically for what they want to find. When you combine between three to five or more words in your key phrases, you expose your site to more potential traffic. A long-tail keyword is simply a key phrase with many words in it. Choose words that describe your services with different combinations.

The use of a long-tail keyword narrows down the specific search for a potential client. As clients get closer and closer to what "it is" that they are looking for, they use more words to describe it in the search engine. If you are using the same long-tail keyword on your webpage and none of your competitors are using that same keyword then you are going to get 100 percent of that traffic.

Create Your Video with
the Software of Your Choice

After completing the outline and design of your video script you're ready to begin production of the video. It is best to hire a professional to produce your videos, however if you are tight on funds than this can easily be completed in-house with free or paid software.

Windows Movie Maker is a popular free video software included with older Windows operating systems and available for free download with current versions. This popular software is user friendly and is capable of producing high quality results. Depending upon the type of video you are producing, it can be as simple as importing images, clips and music. You can also use Google Picasa or animoto.com.

Simple Video Production Instructions

Gather the images and music clips that you plan to use and set them up as you would a slide show. Add the text that includes content that flows naturally and will catch the attention of your audience as well as search engine indexing processes. You can also add a narrative explanation for each image that or clip that is displayed if you don't have speech in the audio. There are plenty of free music clips available on the Internet that allow free non-commercial use.

Cheryl Says:

NOTE: Commercial use will more often than not require a fee. Check the terms of service on the website from which you download clips to make sure that you are complying with copyright and licensing requirements. Just because a website states that a clip is free to download does not mean that it is free for commercial use.

If you are making a video for YouTube, be sure that you check out the AudioSwap feature to double check that the music you use is licensed for use on their site. Here are the instructions for creating a promotional video using Windows Movie Maker.

1. Get to Know the Program

Familiarize yourself with the Windows Movie Maker software if you haven't already. The Task Area provides a list of all of the actions that you will be using in video creation. The Collection Area is where your images and audio will be stored along with special effects that you can implement to enhance your video. The Preview Box allows you to monitor your progress and check your results before finalizing. The Timeline shows you the components of video while you are assembling and editing them so you can see what they look like as you go.

2. Gather Images

Gather your images for the video and go to the Task Area. click on "Import Pictures." Select the images to be imported for the video. Add them in the order that they will appear in the video. This adds them to the Collection Area for further use.

3. Select Audio Files

In the Task Area, choose the "Import Audio/Music" link. Select the audio files that you want to import for your video. After selecting, they will also appear in the Collection Area with the images that you have saved.

4. Build Your Video

You will now locate the music file to be used in the Collection Area. Drag this to the middle bar located on the Timeline and labeled "Audio/Music." The title of the track will appear after you drop the file there.

5. Create Your Title Card

Create your title card which will be the first thing that your viewers see. Click on the "Make Titles or Credits" choice in the Task Area. This opens up the Title Selection page. Select the "Add title at the beginning of the movie" option. From there you'll be taken to the Title Creation screen. Type in the title text and then you'll see it appear in the Preview Box. Look to the left of the screen and you'll find options that allow you to "Change the animation" and "Change the text font and color." Make any needed adjustments in this area. You'll see the edits appear in the Preview Box. When you're satisfied with your edits, click the "Done, add title to movie" option under the text box.

6. Add Your Images

Go to the Collection Area and drag the first image to the timeline and drop it in after the Title Card. You'll see it appear after the Title. Go to the Task Area and click on the "Make Titles or Credits" option again to create a title that shows up between the opening title card and the first image.

7. Add Additional Titles

You can add more titles for the images that are selected if you desire. To do so, choose the link that says "Add title before the selected clip in the timeline." Select the animation and text editing features, make changes and preview them. When you're satisfied with the results, click on the "Done, add title to movie" option.

8. *Add Text*

Add text over the images if desired. Click the "Make Titles or Credits" link and choose "Add title on the selected clip in the timeline" option. Type in your text, make editing changes, then select "Done." Continue with this process until you have added all of the images you want in your video. You can press the play button on the Preview Box to check your progress as you go.

Note: *Don't forget to save your work periodically*

9. *Add Effects and Transitions*

Add effects and transitions to your video if desired. This is done by clicking on the "Show Storyboard" button that is located on the right above the Timeline. Go to the Task Area and click on "View video effects." You'll see a listing of different effects that you can add to your video. Drag the one that you want to use to the Star that is located in the lower left corner of the image on the Storyboard. The Preview Box allows you to see how it looks before you finalize the additions.

10. Add End Credits

Go to the Task Area and click on the "Show collections option. Add the end credits if desired to our video. Click on the "Make Titles or Credits link and choose the "Add credits to the end of the movie" option. Enter the text, use the tools provided to add effects and transitions, preview your work, make any needed edits and when satisfied, click "Done, add title to movie" option.

11. Save Your Video

In the Task Area, click on "Save to my computer." A wizard will open and allow you to select the location and name that you wish to see your video under. You will also have options to set the output format desired. You can also adjust the playback quality. Click Next for a screen that shows the progress of your video as it is being completed. When the process has been completed click "Finish." Your video is now ready for uploading to different social media sites.

VENUES FOR PLACING YOUR VIDEO

There are several different social media sites that you can and should use to drive massive amounts of traffic to your site. The more you choose, the wider your coverage area. Most require you to set up a free account and a home page. The Golden 5 social media sites are Facebook, Twitter, Pinterest, LinkedIn, and Google+. Each has its own set of rules that you must follow along with specialized marketing tools that help you to further optimize the promotion of your video and site. To maximize the effectiveness in using your video to drive web traffic to your site, take advantage of all of the marketing tools that they have to offer you.

Learning how to create a powerful video may seem like a complicated process at first glance, but when you complete the process in a step by step manner, attending to all of the important details as you go, it actually becomes more fun than work. This guide has been designed to walk you through each step of the process and help you to understand the importance of SEO elements into your promotional video. The effort and care that you put into the creation of your video from the basic design and content creation, through the final and completed project will be visible to viewers. After completing the process once, you'll be able to more quickly and easily create new and updated versions that improve with time and experience.

Video Marketing and
the Smart Business Owner

Video marketing is a powerful means of getting your advertising message out to the right viewers. Producing a high quality video that is fully Search Engine Optimized will increase your search engine results rankings and visitor traffic. There are free options, however any smart business owner knows that hiring a videographer and leveraging your time is the best approach to producing high quality videos that best represent your business.

CHAPTER 8 NOTES

What I Learned:

_____

_____

_____

_____

_____

_____

_____

_____

_____

_____

_____

_____

_____

3 Things For Me To Implement From This Chapter:

_____

_____

_____

_____

_____

_____

3 Tasks For Delegation:

_____

_____

_____

_____

_____

_____

1 Question For Cheryl:

_____

_____

_____

"It's not the strongest of species who survive,

nor the most intelligent, but the one most

responsive to change."

~Charles Darwin

CHAPTER 9: SOCIAL MEDIA STRATEGY

Social Media Marketing (SMM) is an essential element to any marketing plan. Without it, you will miss out on opportunities to increase awareness, build fan followings, or drum up business amongst the millions of people using different Social Media like Facebook, Twitter, LinkedIn, Pinterest and Google+. However, to convert Social Media users into paying clients, you cannot randomly post messages on Facebook and then disappear. You have to consistently engage users to develop a rapport, to build trust and to develop a relationship. You also cannot always self-promote because people will begin to ignore you.

Step 1 - Target Your Audience

Understand your target audience. Spend time researching and studying them in order to reach them effectively. Get to know their likes and dislikes, concerns etc. Be sure to spend time learning about your target market before you try to market to them on social media. If you don't understand your target market and then you try to market to them, you will never reach them with your marketing message.

Cheryl Says:

It is important to pay close attention to the way that your potential clients use social media before you begin to advertise or place content on them. More importantly, you have to have a strategy in place to target and convert users. Without a cohesive Social Media Marketing strategy, converting these social media users into clients is simply impossible.

Step 2 - Choose Your Social Networks

There are many networking platforms that your potential clients are currently using. To effectively convert users into consumers, you need to know which platform or platforms are engaging the attention of your potential clients, so that you can craft an effective Social Media Marketing strategy.

Pinterest is a surprisingly good source of traffic and should not be ignored for your business. You want to make sure to maximize social media posts on all five of these websites and be consistent in your posting. We use the HootSuite Enterprise platform to manage our clients social media posts efficiently. There is a pro version that is free (or costs about 20 dollars a month here recently) and I highly recommend that if you manage your own social media, that you use HootSuite to automate your posts. This will allow you to pick a day, like Sunday, to schedule all your posts for the week and respond to all comments from the week before. You can use this same day to schedule your blog posts and then use it to schedule the sharing of those blog posts shortly after they are scheduled to post.

Step 3 - Using Cohesive Marketing

Developing an intelligent and strategic plan is good but it is important to have a cohesive marketing team execute the plan. Co-ordinate with your team, make sure each member knows their role and responsibility, the platform they are handling, and the goals they need to achieve.

If you do not have a team, then make sure that you write down your plan and use some type of automation software to accomplish all the tasks that you must complete each week. We use InfusionSoft to manage all of our client accounts in-house and it works very well for maintaining contact with large numbers of clients. For example, in InfusionSoft, you can set up birthday campaigns to automatically send out birthday cards according to the birthday stored in the system. You can also have the system send emails, faxes, schedule phone calls, and a multitude of other tasks based on specific client behavior.

When setting up automation, it is important to consider client behavior. When a client fills out a particular form, the system can be programmed to automatically email that client, email you, send out a notification to a third-party fulfillment house, and then schedule a phone call follow-up a week later. This is just one example in how a system can be set up to perform much more complex automated tasks.

If you're interested in InfusionSoft, please use the contact information at the end of this book to get in touch with us. We work closely with InfusionSoft in setting up new clients on their system and it will cost you much less (in time and money) to go through us than it will to set up InfusionSoft on your own. I will tell you from experience that InfusionSoft is a very complex system and will take much of your time to set up.

Even if you do not contact us, it is in your best interest to contact a company familiar with InfusionSoft to set it up for you. Unless you have one or two employees that you can dedicate specifically to setting up the system, it is in your best interest to have a company set it up for you rather than try to do this yourself. I'm in no way trying to discourage you from using the system. I highly recommend that you do use it. Once it is set up it will work wonders for your business. I just want make sure that you understand that setting up a system such as InfusionSoft requires a high financial and time investment on your part. For other business types, this may not be an issue. But, when you're a one-man show or only have one or two employees, this is going to take up some time in the initial set-up stages.

Step 4 - Leverage Your Content Management

Set aside a time slot to develop and source relevant content or images to engage users on different Social Media Marketing platforms. This content should include a variety of topics from current trends within the industry to original topics. Pre-schedule content - tweets, pins and posts if possible to prevent 'no post' days due to busy schedules. Also keep in mind that posting content is not enough. If you wish to convert users into clients you need to engage them and build trust. Allocate a dedicated system to respond to comments and conduct discussions. This will serve as a client relationship mechanism that not only builds relationships with potential clients but also manages any potential negative feedback.

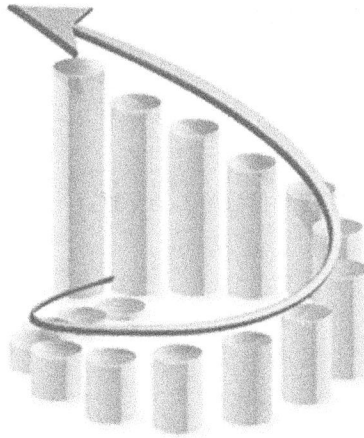

Step 5 - Evaluate Performance Goals

Regularly analyze and evaluate your plan to ensure that your strategy is effective and is engaging your target audience. Use metrics to verify if promotions and activities are running effectively. If they aren't, evaluate the activity, understand the reason behind non-performance, eliminate if required and adjust your strategy accordingly.

Always make sure to track all of your efforts and analyze results on a consistent basis. This is especially true when you're paying for advertising or promotions. You want to make sure that every dollar you spend on marketing comes back in the form of a return on investment.

Leverage The GOLDEN 5 Social Media To Attract And Maintain Loyal Clients And Turn Them Into Raving Fans

Operating a successful business is extremely different today than it was 20 or 30 years ago. Decades ago, people read the newspaper, clipped a coupon, and headed out the door with coupon in hand. Changing trends in social constructs has set this age of marketing apart from all others. Our newspapers are digital, coupons can be shown on your mobile phone, and people can shop from home.

You potential clients now think differently because of the advances in technology and the ways that we communicate through social media. These new 'social norms' reach into the marketing of your services.

The fact is that Internet businesses have become the new 'go to' for fast and convenient shopping. Even brick and mortar businesses who wish to remain competitive must also offer a company website with online ordering to meet client expectations. Attorneys are now faced with the task of getting the attention of their target audience by driving traffic to their websites as quickly as possible.

Social Media Marketing
(Using the Golden Five)

Social media has connected people with varied interests and numerous problems that need solving throughout the world. It has opened up a vast audience of potential clients for businesses that market on the Internet. Merely advertising your business may net a few visitors to your site, but there are a few strategies that you can employ to set the stage for attracting targeted visitors to your site, converting them into clients, stimulating a sense of loyalty and giving them reason to become fans and followers that will help to promote your business. This process takes time and effort that will pay off when done correctly. One of the major advantages of social media marketing is that your information is highly visible to a global audience and it makes your business easier to find locally.

NOTE: Avoid the SHOTGUN Approach

The shotgun approach to advertising may work for some but it is never the most effective approach. If you are marketing to everyone, then you are marketing to no one. If businesses advertised their products to every person on social media, many people would become annoyed and consider the ads to be spam. In a way, they are right. What you find to be necessary advertising for your business, someone else may find to be nothing but spam in their Facebook timeline.

Creating content and a marketing strategy that reaches out to people who have an interest in your services will drive traffic that is more apt to convert them to clients. Some things to consider are the gender, age groups, shopping habits, and social behaviors of the people in this group.

If you want to determine your target audience, look at your last ten clients. What age group are they in? What do they read? What are they interested in? If you don't know, ask them. Send a quick survey out to your last 5 clients and ask them these questions. Ask them how they found you (if you don't already know) and inquire as to what information helped them to make the decision to hire you.

Build Your Social Media Sharing Strategy Correctly to Drive Traffic to Your Site

Your social media sharing should contain important elements to be the most effective in attracting visitors for the conversion process. The shared content should be consistent, interesting and offer solutions for your potential clients' particular needs.

Your shares and posts should begin with a powerful title that gives viewers a sense of the authority in the topic you will discuss. The first few lines need to grab their attention and hold it. Craft the words so they build a need and provide the solution. Appealing to the emotions in a positive manner will draw more traffic than merely stating what you do and how you can be contacted.

Through each phase of social media strategy development you are laying the foundation for an exceptionally effective client acquisition strategy that can be easily implemented when done one step at a time.

Connect With Your Followers

Connecting with followers helps you to establish a relationship with them and assists in the process of conversion from follower to client and then to loyal client, fan and promotional asset for your business (referrals). Always provide your Facebook contact information so they can like your business page and share this information with their social networks. Regularly post new and exciting content that people will enjoy reading and sharing. Be careful to customize the posts to meet the needs and interests of your target audience. Follow up on responses and comments to your posts regularly. This helps followers who like your content to bond with you and become loyal fans of your business.

Cheryl Says:

If you don't have time to post blogs or write content, then hire someone to do it for you. If you don't have time to follow up on social media, then hire someone to do it for you. But, whatever you do, make sure you connect with your visitors and establish a relationship online. If you don't do this, then your competition will.

Use the Marketing Tools Provided by Your Golden Five Social Media Sites

Facebook, Twitter, Pinterest, Linkedin and Google all provide analytical and other tools that will help you to effectively build your following, or audience. These tools can help you to track the number of visitors that you get on particular posts with information about the demographics and possible behaviors of the visitors.

Always use the analytic tools available to you to determine which posts get the most positive responses. This will help you to know which strategies work best with specific groups of people. You can then target these groups with a particular type of advertising and information. This technique is especially useful when your target audience includes a broad range of people.

Create Targeted Posts

After you've established the needs of a few different groups, then target your posts specifically for each of them. Appeal to the problems they share in common and provide the solutions. By targeting your posts you are tailoring the message to be most appealing to certain groups within your target area.

Remember, you may be marketing the same services but alter the message and the presentation in ways that are more interesting to the individual visitors. You not only appeal to potential clients with targeted messages, but as they respond to your message, it is being shared with those in their social media network. People like to do business with people they like. In today's society, people also like to do business with people that *their friends like.*

Contagious Messages

Let your clients know what excites you about your services. When your posts are presented in an excited tone, your clients will feel this vibe. Whatever the emotions are that you express through the tone of your posts, they will be felt by your readers. Let your viewers know that you are excited about your business and about the advantages that your products provide for clients. Any time you show emotion to followers in how a service can make their lives better, you catch their attention.

Use Visual Media on Social Networks

Visual media is important in generating the best tone and message possible. Research has proven that the mind works in images. This can help you to project the personality of your business and make it more inviting and appealing to followers and potential clients alike. Pictures and video clips are useful in delivering a stronger message. It can also reinforce the unique brand of your business and help to make it more memorable in the minds of your potential clients.

USE VISUAL MEDIA

Develop an Offline Loyalty Program

Yes, professionals should have an offline loyalty program. This should be a newsletter advertised on your website that is mailed to potential, previous, and present clients at a physical address. Promote it on your website and on social media.

Mailing a physical newsletter helps to build both loyalty and repeat business. When a client feels that they know you and that you've treated them with excellent service, then they are more likely to positively promote your business. Sending them monthly newsletters keeps you at the forefront of their mind. This works for all past and present clients. Smart lawyers know that just because they just helped a client doesn't necessarily mean that they don't have a friend with a similar issue. Criminal lawyers know that people in trouble with the law may tend to have friends that possibly have some trouble with the law. Family attorneys know that legal issues concerning families are emotional and a happy client will tell everyone and their brother (pun intended) about their experience. Why let the service that you have provided fade in their memory? Send them a newsletter every month and keep your name in front of them for future referrals.

*VIP members have access to discounted pricing on done-for-you newsletters. Contact your SIMC Team at **SIMCcorp.com** or call (866) 986-5650.*

Keep Content Fresh and Updated

Add valuable information and content to your website or blog on a regular basis. Consistency will increase client confidence and help them to remain interested in visiting your site. Keep your posts interesting and stimulating to the readers so they will respond to and spread the word about your business message.

Your posts will be seen by others in their news feeds and can more easily catch the eyes of interested parties. Never allow your content to become stale or boring. If you're not getting the responses or likes that you are pleased with, then change your strategy. When possible, expand your posts and shares to meet the needs and expectations of your potential clients. If your sharing strategy is not consistently evolving in ways that will keep your current clients satisfied and new clients coming in, it is time to give it an update. Make the content appropriate for those in your client base and for those you hope to attract to your site.

Convert Social Media Followers

There are many ways to use the Golden 5 social media sites to attract visitors to your site. Targeted visitors who are the most apt to convert to clients are exposed to your page with the initial relationship offered through social media.

The conversion process from follower to client will depend upon the quality of the content and services that you provide. Offer high quality content that is packed with useful information and that shows how your business can benefit them. Happy clients who comment on the excellence of your service and how your business helped them will drive more traffic to your site. These raving fans help to bring more targeted referrals to your website than any other form of advertising could possibly bring.

Consistently use social media posts and conversations to interact with your clients and keep them interested in and engaged with your business. Providing your clients with excellence in client service and consistent interaction through social media will generate continued interest in your site and turn clients into loyal fans and create sources of future referrals for your business.

CHAPTER 9 NOTES

What I Learned:

_____

_____

_____

_____

_____

_____

_____

_____

_____

_____

_____

_____

_____

3 Things For Me To Implement From This Chapter:

_____

_____

_____

_____

_____

_____

3 Tasks For Delegation:

_____

_____

_____

_____

_____

_____

1 Question For Cheryl:

_____

_____

_____

"People influence people. Nothing influences people more than a recommendation from a trusted friend. A trusted referral influences people more than the best broadcast message. A trusted referral is the Holy Grail of advertising"

~ Mark Zuckerberg

CHAPTER 10: PUBLICITY ADVERTISING

You do not have to be a content expert to recognize that 'content is king' on the Internet. In fact, content marketing has come full circle since 1996 when Bill Gates wrote his essay "Content is King," proclaiming his excitement that anyone with Internet access can publish content. With so much published content on the Internet, it is now more fittingly stated that content has become somewhat of a challenge for anyone looking to promote their business on the Internet.

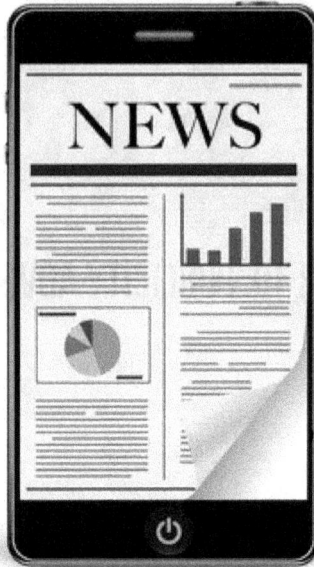

The fact is that the Internet is quickly becoming a content marketing landfill. Although there is, without argument, a lot of great quality content on the Internet, there is also plenty of garbage littering the traffic lanes of the information superhighway. The content police, in the form of search engine giants, spend a bulk of their money and intellect on weeding out the trash and presenting end-users with a flow of quality content. Content needs to remain in that stream of information, and not everyone's does.

The Importance Of Content Marketing In American Consumerism

With quality content filtered in a user-friendly form by search engine companies, it is no surprise that the Internet is quickly becoming a fundamental research tool in the American routine of consumerism. According to the Consumer Barometer, 78 percent of consumers research a product online before purchasing. This means that target markets are reading about, and forming a reputation-based opinion on, business products and services before they make the decision to pull out their credit card.

Even small local businesses need to be cognizant of the importance of quality content. The Consumer Barometer indicates that 38 percent of US consumers research local businesses online to find the products and services they need. Smart legal professionals would be well-advised to ensure that they know what consumers and content channels are saying about them online and then leverage mainstream media to polish the online positioning of their business, products, and services.

Businesses Create Trusted And Quality Content With Publicity Advertising

As the newest trend in online marketing, publicity advertising is the fastest and most reliable way to build a positive reputation and trust for a business in the virtual world of the Internet. It is quickly becoming the smart business owner's most efficient advertising tool because it establishes authority, invites third-party endorsement, ties the business brand to trusted news, and leverages content marketing.

In blunt contrast to the inherent prejudice of self-promotion blogs and fake affiliate marketing articles, publicity advertising communicates the company message with thought influencers, and if done correctly, can make the business voice an influencer in the industry or niche. Additionally, there is high potential for publicity advertising to go viral. According to an article by the Harvard Business Review, massive brand exposure and viral marketing are the ways to break through the infinite noise and clutter of display ads and marketing content.

Leveraging mainstream media unlocks the door to potential for a viral snowball effect. Getting picked up by one or two media outlets can certainly help a business get noticed, but the true miracle occurs when a story gets picked up by multiple news outlets and gets noticed and shared by other news outlets through social media. A company message needs massive, intentional, strategized content marketing to get noticed by multiple news outlets. It takes quality content to get that type of attention from the media.

Effective Publicity Advertising Requires Businesses To Add Value

Even the media is bombarded by hundreds and thousands of pointless press releases from attorneys that mimic each other with 'look at me' company announcements. Getting media attention means providing quality content to mass media influencers. If a company wants media attention, it has to give them something worth the media audiences' attention. But first, the issue is getting noticed through the clutter of poorly-planned content that media contacts already receive (and ignore) on a daily basis.

Cheryl Says:

The fact is that media influencers are not reading your blog -- not yet anyway -- and definitely not without work to get their attention. Media influencers want content that will be interesting and engaging for their audience. A post on your blog, by itself, is not going to attract the type of viral media attention that publicity advertising can attract.

Value-Added Content

Attracts Authoritative Links

Although publicity advertising should not be used solely for search engine optimization or marketing, the resultant media backlinks are an important part of both. Media backlinks should be a byproduct and not an objective. A successful publicity campaign encourages authoritative media outlets to link to content on a business website and this helps both with search engine optimization and driving traffic to a website. These backlinks are of much higher value than that of links coming from less authoritative websites.

Publicity Advertising Side-steps Stigma Of Paid Advertising

A 2006 study from the Journal of Consumer Research shows that even relevant display advertising interrupts a consumer's content consumption and causes a negative experience. A case study example of this is imgur.com. Imgur is a user-based image sharing and voting platform which, according to the Imgur website, is rated by ComScore among the top 100 US sites. Recently, they started allowing paid advertising. The negative reaction by their audience is demonstrated by the advertising fail of the promotion of the 'Legalize Ted' campaign on the storytelling community. The Imgur community's reaction was so negative to the advertising campaign that is spurred an adverse comment frenzy and an anti-Ted sentiment in the community. The community reacted to the breach of trust they felt by the intrusive interruption advertising.

However, the community does not reject all paid advertising. Take this eBay case for example. The advertiser went out of its way to learn the community's customs and had their advertising accepted. eBay integrated itself into the media and was accepted more readily than the blatant interruption advertising that was quickly rejected.

Blatant interruption advertising has the same effect as calling someone at dinnertime and then trying to sell them something. However, it would take an incredible amount of time for a single business owner to learn the customs of several hundred online communities and then try their hand at paid advertising that does not spark a collective revolt within an established community. In contrast, publicity advertising attracts thought leaders within these communities to write about the business and provide third-party endorsement to their audiences. With this approach, the business is not an intrusion in the media, it is accepted as part of the media.

Sway Positive Status And Trust For Business With Publicity Advertising

According to an analysis on journalism.org there are striking differences in the way that consumers receive their news depending on their political affiliations. The analysis indicates that although consistent conservatives distrust most media, they rely on a handful of news sources that they trust. A large percentage of consistent conservatives - 88 percent - trust Fox news. Whereas, consistent liberals trust a much larger mix of news from CNN, MSNBC, New York Times, BuzzFeed, PBS, BBC, Huffington Post, Washington Post and many more. It is also interesting to note that the analysis found that 81 percent of liberals distrust Fox news and 75 percent distrust the Rush Limbaugh show.

The Wall Street Journal stands out as the only media source (included in the analysis) found to be more trusted than not by both liberals and conservatives across the board. This indicates that although there are some media that are middle-of-the-road, the vast majority of liberals read more of the news while conservatives tend to watch and listen to the news more regularly. To reach a broader audience, publicity advertising must attract as much of a diverse mix of the media as possible to gain the trust of the target market without alienating one political demographic or the other.

Ideological Placement of Each Source's Audience

Average ideological placement on a 10-point scale of ideological consistency of those who got news from each source in the past week...

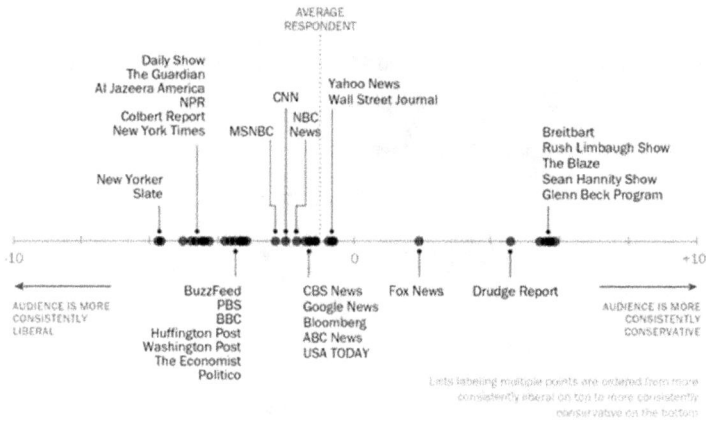

AVERAGE RESPONDENT

Daily Show
The Guardian
Al Jazeera America
NPR
Colbert Report
New York Times

New Yorker
Slate

CNN

MSNBC

NBC
News

Yahoo News
Wall Street Journal

Breitbart
Rush Limbaugh Show
The Blaze
Sean Hannity Show
Glenn Beck Program

-10 0 +10

AUDIENCE IS MORE CONSISTENTLY LIBERAL

BuzzFeed
PBS
BBC
Huffington Post
Washington Post
The Economist
Politico

CBS News
Google News
Bloomberg
ABC News
USA TODAY

Fox News

Drudge Report

AUDIENCE IS MORE CONSISTENTLY CONSERVATIVE

Lists labeling multiple points are ordered from more consistently liberal on top to more consistently conservative on the bottom.

American Trends Panel (wave 1). Survey conducted March 19-April 29, 2014. Q22. Based on all web respondents. Ideological consistency based on a scale of 10 political values questions (see About the Survey for more details.) ThinkProgress, DailyKos, Mother Jones, and The Ed Schultz Show are not included in this graphic because audience sample sizes are too small to analyze.

PEW RESEARCH CENTER

Source: Journalism.org

Publicity Advertising Encourages Social Sharing Beyond Mass Media

According to Pew Research, 90 percent of Americans own a cell phone and 42 percent own a tablet. But what is really interesting is the deeper research that shows 67 percent of cell phone owners check their phone for messages, alerts, and calls, even when there is no phone notification. Moreover, 44 percent sleep with their phone to avoid missing smartphone notifications.

So, despite the research that shows that audiences despise interruption marketing, it seems that Americans crave interruption. The trick is to become the interruption that they crave. With Publicity Advertising, the business gains a better chance of becoming that 'welcome notification' across the target consumer's smartphone. When 'advertising' becomes news from a source they trust and crave, viewers are more apt to share the message with their friends, families, and followers.

Research on Journalism.org shows that 10 percent of smartphone users get their news from Twitter, while 41 percent get news from Facebook. Additionally, 63 percent of users on both platforms use them to get news beyond that of just their friends or family. But if a company is looking to reach more of its target market through news and publicity, then targeting Twitter users will reach more of the target market. This is because 46 percent of Twitter users follow news outlets.

On Facebook and Twitter, More Users Are Getting News

% of users of each platform who get news there

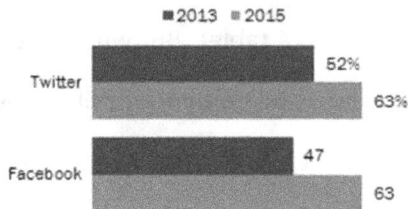

■2013 ■2015

Twitter — 52% / 63%

Facebook — 47 / 63

Social Media and News Survey, March 13-15 & 20-22, 2015. Q2, Q4. Facebook News Survey, Aug. 21-Sept. 2, 2013. Q9.

Note: News is defined as "information about events & issues beyond just your friends and family."

PEW RESEARCH CENTER

Source: Journalism.org

To get a publicity campaign to the Twitter community, a business must get there through the graces of the Twitter influencers that are the news media. With large companies vying for media attention and increasing their content marketing another 58 percent over the next year, attorneys are left wondering how to compete with the noise and clutter. The use of publicity advertising allows smaller businesses to reach the mass media and the thought influencers beyond the media outlets.

Strategizing Publicity Campaigns
for Small Business

There is such an abundance of content published every second of every day that it has become a daunting task to produce the type of quality content that will attract thought influencers to share content. But, this is a double-edged sword to a small business' benefit, because the challenge for both small business and news media is the lack of time to produce enough content to share. A company's competition is likely submitting ill-prepared press releases. So, by a business taking the time and forethought to provide quality content to thought influencers, the business greatly increases the chance of getting their message hand picked out of the stack of press releases.

Though content rules the Internet, simply producing quality content is no longer enough to gain an edge against the competition. Establishing trust and authority with an audience is vital to an effective marketing strategy, and doing so has become increasingly difficult. In the early days of content marketing, the mere existence of consistent content on a website could achieve the following that aspiring marketers dream of earning today. Now that the Internet is somewhere between growth and maturity in its life-cycle, businesses will experience much more success by actively integrating the business into the media through publicity campaigns. These are outlets that target audiences already trust, rather than those any small business could create on its own.

*Visit **TheCelebrityMakers.com** for full-service publicity advertising services that grab media attention and may turn you into the overnight authority in your area of professional legal expertise.*

AS SEEN ON

CBS NEWS   abc   NBC   FOX

Getting seen on mass media gives you the competitive advantage over your competition when you leverage your 'as seen on' logos on your website and social media profiles.

CHAPTER 10 NOTES

What I Learned:

_____

_____

_____

_____

_____

_____

_____

_____

_____

_____

_____

_____

_____

3 Things For Me To Implement From This Chapter:

_____

_____

_____

_____

_____

_____

3 Tasks For Delegation:

_____

_____

_____

_____

_____

_____

1 Question For Cheryl:

_____

_____

_____

"Knowledge comes by taking things apart: analysis. But wisdom comes by putting things together."

~ John A. Morrison

CHAPTER 11: PUTTING IT ALL TOGETHER WITH SIMC

The accumulation of great fortunes calls for POWER, and power is acquired through highly organized and intelligently directed specialized knowledge, but that knowledge does not, necessarily, have to be in the possession of the man who accumulates the fortune.
---Napoleon Hill in Think and Grow Rich

Imagine that you are the most successful professional in your field of expertise; ever. Seriously contemplate the thought. Visualize it. Clients are lining up at your door just for a chance that you might have an opening to accept them as your newest client. Your services are unlike any other professional in your industry and potential clients know it. You have defied all of the odds and you have carved out a name for yourself as the go-to professional. Clients would rather wait months for you to have an opening than hire anybody else.

Then, one morning you wake up at three a.m. in the morning staring at the ceiling. You want to take your dreams of success to the next level, but so much of your time is spent trying to find your next client. You think about how much more you could do, and how much more you could make, if only you had someone to take care of online marketing while you concentrated on your business. You realize that in this dream of being the most successful professional, you were not imagining yourself building your website. You are not learning the next great social network. You are not learning programming or code. In fact, in that dream you are working one-on-one with clients and performing to the peak of your abilities.

Any smart business owner knows that to become successful, you must concentrate on your core business and delegate those tasks that do not make the best use of your time. As a busy professional, your time is not best spent learning how to make a website or market your services online.

The fact is that you wouldn't hire the landscaper to remodel your kitchen. So then why would you hire yourself to strategically market your services on the Internet? How can you ever become the sought-after professional when you are sitting behind a computer trying to learn the best way to use a title Meta-tag and how it affects your SEO? If you already know the best way to use a title Meta-tag, then you have already spent way too much time working in my profession when you could've been making money in your own. Misplacing your energy is talked about as one of the greatest mistakes that all entrepreneurs make before they become successful.

In **Cracking the Millionaire Code**, a book by Mark Victor Hansen and Robert G Allen, the authors discuss how entrepreneurs are so chronically independent that most of us don't look up from our work long enough to ask ourselves if there is an easier or faster way to get where we are going. The authors explain how we are self-reliant to a fault and that we can't seem to delegate those tasks that so desperately need to be delegated. We get so busy and so overwhelmed that we forget that there are much more intelligent ways to run our businesses. We forget about the power of leveraging other's time.

When you imagine yourself as a top performer in your profession, do you see yourself sitting behind a computer in frustration learning how to build a website? Do you see yourself trying to figure out how the last Google algorithm change affected your rankings? Of course not. As entrepreneurs we often forget to work smarter and not harder.

In the **Law of Success** by Napoleon Hill, Napoleon explains that "we are the victims of our habits, no matter who we are or what may be our life-calling." As entrepreneurs we get into the habit of trying to do

STRATEGIC INTERNET MARKETING FOR LEGAL PROFESSIONALS

everything ourselves. We somehow firmly believe that the best way to do anything is to do it ourselves. If you have ever read **Psycho-Cybernetics** by Maxwell Maltz, then you will know the only way to dehypnotize yourself from these false beliefs and bad habits is to concentrate on that which you most desire and form that image clearly in your mind.

Although the entrepreneurial definition of insanity (*doing the same thing over and over and expecting different results*) is one of the most overused clichés, you can't ignore the message. If you want to create positive change in your business, then you need to start by making a change in how you think about your business. Because, if you have read this far, then what you are currently doing in your business is not working. If you have the time to read this book and learn my profession, then you are not spending enough time in your own. It's time to make a change and delegate those tasks which are preventing you from professional success. Is there a legitimate reason that you are taking time away from your profession to perform the tasks associated with another? Or is it just a case of excusitis? David J Schwartz, PhD describes the failure disease, excusitis, in his book, **The Magic of Thinking Big**. "Persons with mediocre accomplishments are quick to explain why they haven't, why they don't, why they can't, and why they aren't."

So, now ask yourself these question. Why are you not as successful

Professional Coaching Members login to *GoSIMC.com* for member templates and videos.

as you have envisioned yourself to be? Have you made one too many excuses? Two? Three? Are your spending too much time on completing tasks that do not make the best use of your time? What is holding you back from the success that will put you forever in front of your competition? The answer is time. Leveraging your use of time.

Winning – playing the game better than your competition and changing the game when necessary – requires finding a new way to sustain organic revenue and profit growth and consistently improve margins.
---A.G. Lafley in The Game Changer

So, Now It Has Come Time for You to Make a Decision

Are you ready to become the professional that has clients lined up at the door awaiting the mere chance of hiring you? Are you ready to defy the odds and carve a name out for yourself in your profession? **Are you ready to apply SIMC: Strategy, Implementation, Magnetism, and Consistency?**

If you are not ready, then stop right here and close this book. **Do not turn to the next page.**

A Special Offer for My Courageous Readers

Congratulations! I knew that you were ready and I am excited for you! Reading this far proves that you are ready to take that next step in your business. You are willing to do what it takes to become the most successful professional that you can become. I know that you are sick and tired of wasting your precious energy on tasks that take away from your core business. If you could just find the time, then you can achieve your dream of becoming the sought-after professional that you know that you can become. And now, you know that to get there you must delegate those tasks that are distracting you from your goals.

So, I extend to you a special offer. I truly want you to make the best decision regarding your time BOTH for you and for your business. Now is the right time for you to make the move from doing everything yourself, to delegating marketing tasks that are draining your time. If not now, then when? You may be currently contemplating the possibility of hiring professional services to market your company online. I would like to extend to you, not one, not two, but THREE separate offers to help you decide the best course of action for your business based entirely on your current situation and where you want to go.

FOR THOSE THAT JUST WANT A PROFESSIONAL OPINION

Offer #1: A 30 Minute One-On-One Competitive Research Analysis of Your Current Online Marketing Opportunities

For up to one half hour, I will personally walk with you through your current online marketing and assess those aspects that may be currently holding you back online. We'll take a peek behind the curtains of your competition and reveal potential marketing opportunities for your business. I will provide a comprehensive Research Analysis on the current rankings of your website in Google and Bing search engine results. We will also go over a competitive analysis of similar websites competing for the same keywords as your website. You also get an in-depth look at key problem areas that may be holding you back from top search engine results in your local area.

There is no obligation whatsoever for this analysis. I am not a salesperson and these are first-come, first-served. I only set aside a few time-slots a week for these, so schedule yours now.

Simply visit GoSIMC.com/bookoffer1

If you would rather call us to schedule this assessment, you may call (866) 986-5650.

FOR SMART PROFESSIONALS THAT ARE READY TO DELEGATE THE TASKS HOLDING THEM BACK FROM SUCCESS

Offer #2: 180 Risk Free Days of Full-Service

VIP Services

If you are ready to have all of your local and online marketing efforts professionally coordinated and aligned to maximize your online presence, then we are ready to prove that we are, *hands-down*, the only choice in Strategic Internet Marketing. By coordinating and aligning all of your local and online marketing efforts, we are able to GUARANTEE that you will be 'head-over-heels' in love with our services! AND we do it all at a fraction of the cost of a full-time employee!

YOUR GUARANTEE: if we do not EXCEED your expectations in the first 180 days of service, FIRE US! And we will return everything the way that it was before we started and REFUND 100 PERCENT OF YOUR SETUP FEES! GUARANTEED!!

Simply visit GoSIMC.com/bookoffer2

If the Research Analysis Session is no longer available at no charge on the website, then please call (866) 986-5650 and mention this book.

FOR THOSE JUST GETTING STARTED OR OTHERWISE FINANCIALLY STRESSED

Offer #3: Scholarship to

Professional Coaching at BBU

If you are not ready to have all of your local and online marketing efforts professionally coordinated and aligned to maximize your online presence, then **Brass Balls University** is the perfect option to get the success ball rolling. As a Professional Coaching member at BBU, you will learn how to implement ALL of the concepts in this book with step-by-step instruction from the professionals at SIMC Corp.

[See Next Page]

Simply visit GoSIMC.com/bookoffer3

Promotion Code: BBULE

The course is normally $1,995, but because you read this far into my book, I will cover $1,798 of your tuition. (You must use the link provided above.)

You may think that this offer is "too good to be true" because of the cost of the course. I assure you that you will pay ONLY $197 for the 8-week course if you use the promotion code I have given you above. Look, not everyone can afford our full-service agency. I get that. So, the only way I can maximize the number of people that we can help to become successful is by giving you the tools you need to help yourself get to the level where you *can* afford to allow us to help you.

Why? Well, if someone gifted you this book or if you purchased this book yourself, then you ARE our target market. Some businesses spend hundreds of thousands of dollars in marketing to reach their target market. I already have my book in your hands. So, if it costs me $1,798 to get you to the point where you can afford us, then we both win. You become more successful and we gain a new client. When you are ready, and as our full-service client, your life-time value over the next 5, 10, or 20 years makes my initial investment in you irrelevant. The offer is genuine, and I highly suggest you get started right now while it is fresh in your mind.

ABOUT THE AUTHOR

Cheryl Waller, BSB/MKT, MBA, is a Marketing Strategist for highly successful professionals. A US Navy Veteran, she is the president and founder of SIMC Corp, a marketing firm specializing in providing Internet marketing solutions for busy professionals that want to dominate their local geographic area, leverage their business, and live the life of their dreams. She lives in Vero Beach Florida with her fiancé, Daniel, her youngest of three boys, Nicholas, and her dog, an American Staffordshire Terrier named Blue.

REASONS 'WHY'

Having raised three boys as a single mother for the majority of their lives, I would like to share my reasons 'why' with you. The top two pictures on the following page are placed there simply because the oldest two boys (now both in their 20's) asked me not to put them in the book. I had them take pictures with Santa for years after most boys would have stopped obliging their mother's requests for pictures with Santa. The pages that follow that are just a few of my favorites photos and represent my reasons 'why'. When we start a business, we all have our 'whys' for what we do.

Please share Your reasons 'why' on our Facebook page https://www.facebook.com/strategicimcorp with the hashtag #WhySIMC and I will do my best to share each year's Santa photos. (If the boys don't kill me for putting these pics in here)

Christmas 2007: Cheryl, Nicholas, Santa, Bryan, and Michael

Christmas 2013 Michael, Santa, Nicholas, Bryan

Cheryl's Granddaughter, Aubrielle, Christmas 2014

Cheryl & Her Dad, Thomas Mizzles 1976

Cheryl, US Navy, 2002

Bryan JROTC 2011

Nicholas at Universal Studios 2013 (The look on his face AFTER the picture,

when he realized what was behind him, was awesome)

Bryan & Nicholas- Mud Jam 2013

(That Ford Probe they are standing on is Bryan's little rebel car that 'could'. He drove that thing all over the fairgrounds and didn't get stuck in the mud once. If you have ever been to a mud jam, then you understand that even big trucks get pulled out of the mud regularly at these events. That car was pretty awesome!)

BLUE'S AWESOME STORY

Hey! Shhhhhh... Don't tell Mom that I slipped my story in here just before the book went to print. My name is Blue, I am in charge of Security and Floor Duty at SIMC, and this is my story!

I was born to a beautiful blue-eyed, dark-brindle American Stafford-shire Terrier in Rosebud, TX. When my adoptive Mom picked me and my brother Maximus out of the litter at 6 weeks of age, I had beautiful bright blue eyes. That's why she named me Blue. The blue eyes turned to hazel, but Mom was nice enough to let me keep my name Blue and not change it to a girl's name. My brother and I spent the first few months of our lives in Killen, TX just outside of the Fort Hood Army Base. It was nice there. We used to spend a lot of time at the creek playing in the water and chasing these slippery little underwater things that Mom called fish. Then, she moved us to Florida where we found out that water stands up and chases you! She calls it the beach. It looks kind of like the creek we used to go to, but it's bigger and has a lot more sand. I get to chase the water and run from it when it chases me. I like Florida water! It is way more fun!

Although many people confuse me with a 'pit bull', I am an American Staffordshire terrier. My breed is of the mastiff terrier family (and at 90lbs I weigh more than double the Pit Bull Terrier weight). I found it hard to find a job because I am kind of lazy. People seem to want me to do something and all I ever really want to do is sleep. I have even had some people throw yellow round things and ask me to go get it for them. (And I'm the one that's lazy? Sheesh! You threw it. You get it!) I mean, I love the beach and I am up for a car ride anytime, but my main gig is sleeping and no one wanted to pay me to do that.

That's when I discovered SIMC Corp. You see, Mom owns this business where she stares at a computer screen all day making tapping sounds with her fingers. She took me with her to work one day and it turns out they needed someone to hold the floor down. Perfect! I settled right into my new job at SIMC Corp and although I am only here part-time, it is the perfect place for me to keep an eye on Mommy while I make my rounds holding down the floor next to everyone's desks. I take my job seriously, so I have to make sure that everyone's floor gets the same amount of attention during the day. Mom said something about security duty. I like that too! It's this thing where everyone that walks in the door must immediately pet me. Between that and all the treats everyone slips me under the desks, I am living the life!

Thanks for reading! Time for a nap now!

- Blue

MORE REASONS 'WHY' – IN THEIR OWN WORDS

The following pages are testimonials from clients that I have had the privilege of working with over the many years that I have worked in Internet marketing. Many are current clients, many are past clients, some are clients for which I worked in a limited capacity as a freelancer and yet others are from my brief time in the corporate world. But all of these reasons 'why' are in their own words. These testimonials can all be verified by visiting my LinkedIn profile page: **LinkedIn.com/in/cherylwaller**

NOTE: None of the testimonials were in exchange for any sort of compensation whatsoever. Some spelling & grammar corrections have been made and the names of some companies have been removed for privacy or personal reasons.

As a lifelong resident of and Real Estate Agent in Greater Tampa Bay, I put my insider knowledge to work for you and assist you with area home buying & selling.

Joe LoCicero 🐦 @54realty
☎ (813) 435 – 5411

Joseph LoCicero

Broker Associate Tampa Florida

www.54Realty.com

❝❝ *Cheryl is fantastic and handles all of my SEO and social media sites. She constantly keeps me relevant and does a fantastic job. Her client service is superb and she is quick to jump on any task at hand. I'd highly recommend using her services. You will find great value.*

> When I say that my Houses are Rockin' 'cuz the Buyers are Knocking', it is more than just another 'tag-line'. I have that extra bit of rock-n-roll rhythm that no other agent has!
>
> Gary Rossignol 🐦 @GaryRossignol
> ☎ (513) 777-2402

Gary Rossignol

Cincinnati Rock-n-Roll Real Estate Agent

www.PriceLineHomes.com

" *Cheryl has the creative juices to make my website stand out from all others. She learned all about me and designed the perfect website and keeps it going especially with all the ongoing changes that are needed along the way. Cheryl is the BEST!*

> Brian Mallonee is a take-charge advocate and a well-disciplined trial lawyer. He has defended thousands of cases and has extensive experience in all phases of the criminal justice system.
>
> Brian Mallonee ☎ (772) 464 - 1991

Brian Mallonee

Law Office of Brian H. Mallonee

www.StLucieCriminalLaw.com

" *Cheryl is a detail-oriented SEO and SEM expert. She gives you personalized attention and understands the nuances of her chosen profession, including keeping up to date on the latest algorithms the search engines are looking for. I recommend her work.*

Michael Ferguson has represented buyers and sellers in the Palm Beaches for over 15 years. Prior to his career in real estate Michael was a Military Escort to Presidents Reagan and Bush.

Michael Ferguson 🐦 @stuartproperty
☎ (561) 222 - 1850

Michael Ferguson

Broker, Edgewater Property and Realty, LLC

www.EdgewaterPR.com

" *I hired Cheryl to create an online presence for me and my website. Wow... She not only was very creative but amazingly fast. Within a couple days I was right up where I needed to be. I recommend her to anyone and everyone I know.*

Sandy has been shooting on-time and on-budget with Award-Winning Advertising Photography services for discriminating graphic designers and art directors since 1971.

Sandy Levy ☎ (305) 262 - 9229

Sandy Levy

Visual Impact Photography, Miami Florida

www.LevyPhoto.com

" *Cheryl was extremely helpful with me on the phone when I called her asking questions about marketing my business. Cheryl was very patient with me, was of great help, and took plenty of time to carefully explain various options. I can fully recommend Cheryl with no reservation whatsoever.*

Yes I'm a bit eccentric! A long time Internet Pro who loves to cook, cut the rug on the dance floor & advise investors with buying killer FL rental properties!

Agi Anderson 🐦 @eproagi
☎ (321) 698 - 0021

Agi Anderson
Internet Marketing / Investment Property Pro
eProAgi.com

" *Cheryl Waller brings new meaning to "exceeding one's expectations." Her knowledge and capability with blogs, websites and social media coupled with her creative ability, results with a final product beyond outstanding. Cheryl is extremely talented, but what truly impressed me the most-- she delivers so much more than what's expected!! I highly recommend Cheryl Waller.*

Integrated direct response integrated fundraising professional. Editor of the Healthcare Fundraising Blog.

Rick Christ 🐦 @FundraisingRick
☎ 540-239-6497

Rick Christ
Writer, Speaker, Consultant

❝ *We turned to Cheryl for a custom Facebook tab for a client. She quickly understood the objectives, helped improve the design, let us know what changes were afoot with Facebook, and delivered a better-than-we-expected project, on time and on budget! We're eager to use her services again.*

Coach Light Real Estate LLC. has gained a well–deserved reputation as a top Eustis real estate brokerage company.

Dave Morehead ☎ 352-483-6083

Dave Morehead
Broker - Coach Light Real Estate, LLC
CoachLightRealEstate.com

❝ *Cheryl is an incredible teacher/trainer. Her marketing expertise is nationally recognized and she is one of the most detail oriented people I have ever worked with. She truly cares about her job and her clientele.*

We are dual citizen/resident Real Estate
Professionals providing Phoenix Real Estate &
Calgary Real Estate services to fellow
Canadians and Americans.

Laurie Lavine 🐦 @lavineteam
☎ 888-494-8558

Laurie Lavine - The Lavine Team
Canada to Phoenix Real Estate
AlbertaToPhoenix.com

" *Cheryl Waller is a tremendous resource for any professional that wants to increase their marketing presence through social networking and search engine optimization of blogs, websites, etc. Her knowledge, advice and creativity will propel your business if you implement her suggestions and hire her to create business website pages for you.*

20 Year Print & Digital Media veteran specializing in emerging virtual tour technology and helping clients navigate the digital marketing landscape.

John Varnedore
☎ (501) 520-1815

John Varnedore
Impact 360 Media
www.Impact360Media.com

" " Top notch with great marketing ideas!

I'm here to help you make a difference & be your happiest, wisest & most financially secure self. Write info@themachreegroup.com.

Cree Quaker 🐦 @creequaker
☎ (845) 679-1237

Cree Quaker
The Machree Group, Kingston NY
TheMachreeGroup.com

❝ *Cheryl has great marketing strategies that have been increasing my business' visibility and bottom-line!*

Anthony Castelli is a highly regarded personal injury trial lawyer in Cincinnati serving clients throughout Ohio for over 34 years. He has been listed as an Ohio Super Lawyer and fights with all his heart to get injury victims full compensation.

Anthony Castelli 🐦 @castellilaw
☎ (513) 621-2345

Anthony Castelli
Cincinnati Accident & Injury Attorney
CastelliLaw.com

" *I met Cheryl over the Internet. She responded immediately to what I needed. She put up a great custom Facebook page for my attorney business page. She also volunteered other things to help me with social media marketing. I expect to have a long term relationship with her and highly recommend her marketing expertise.*

Emily Lebow - Residential Real Estate

" I met Cheryl online from a prominent Naples Realtor who was generous enough to share Cheryl's name with me. I so appreciate her responsiveness and talent and willingness to go the extra mile. She is a true professional. I have since recommended Cheryl to my friends who need SEO or Social Networking help. She's the best!

Otto Strunk - RN at North Shore University Hospital

" Cheryl has great ideas and has the knowledge and ability to put those ideas into actions. I highly recommend her!!!

Darryl Hill Coldwell Banker Residential

" Cheryl comes highly recommended, always gets back to me promptly, great communication!

Ginny Lee, Realtor, CRS, ABA,

"Cheryl is great to work with...everything she does is so creative and I love it. She has done fan pages and websites and everything for me! I will keep working with her and hope you do to...She is the BEST!

Angela Johnson Co-Founder, Market Me Mobile-ly VP, J Philip Real Estate LLC

" I don't know of any other person I could so glowingly recommend as such an invaluable resource in the field of developing one's social media marketing profile. The breadth and depth of her areas of expertise are extremely impressive and she manages to structure the project as a manageable progression.

Sydney Chase Sr Founder/President SydChaseGroupLLC Author (No Bull Real Estate)

" *Cheryl is a great person to work with, I have worked with her on a few occasion and plan to have her do more work for all 5 of our companies. She is very easy to get along with and is very hands on. Thanks Cheryl – Syd*

Santiago Arvizu - Social Media Marketing

" *Good professional experience. I recommend her.*

Tim Owens - Owner, Central Florida Mortgage

" *Cheryl is very concerned about time and deadlines and reminds the client of the same. She is very professional and I would recommend her to anyone!*

 *Avril Anjers- Mountain Light Real Estate*

" *I've had the pleasure of working with Cheryl and recently I hired her to help me with my Facebook page. She is an expert in Social Media and a her Facebook fan pages are a cut above. She took my vision and made it a reality. She brings professionalism, expertise, and a wealth of knowledge to all she does.*

 *Bart Wilson - VPiX sales / marketing rock star.*

" *Cheryl is certainly the "digital diva," of online marketing from Facebook fan pages to helping her clients understand how to make sense of the "blogoshphere." Her "can do," attitude is certainly refreshing. And she knows her stuff. Really. Tenacious and hardworking ***** Five Stars.*

David Hagler - Dave's Dirtworks & Landscape

Cheryl is the person for you! She constructed my webpage on Facebook and did a great job. Cheryl has many good ideas and is always willing to listen to my many challenges on the web. She is in tune with networking on the social networks and on the web as well. I highly recommend Cheryl for any of your marketing needs.

John Cobb - Realtor

Cheryl created my Facebook Fan Page. She did a terrific job and designed it just the way I requested. Cheryl is very knowledgeable on Internet marketing, Web design, and a SEO expert. Cheryl is very fast, friendly, and reliable.

Jennifer Young - REO Listing Agent/Short Sale Specialist for VA, MD & DC

" It was great to work with Cheryl on my team's Facebook page. We had some trouble in the beginning with our local rep, but Cheryl was able to step in and work it all out in a professional manner - giving me lots of options. Thanks Cheryl.

Troy Williams - President at Verified Safe

" I have hired many people in my 18 years being on the Internet to do special type works and found that none can hold the level of Cheryl she is very good at what she does when it comes to anything about blogging and copy and creativity. I would highly recommend her for anything dealing with Internet marketing

Eric Rosen - Internet Marketing Specialist

" " Cheryl is a great resource when looking to have a web site or social media site built from scratch, or even consulting with you to explain what changes need to be made for maximum success. She really impressed me with her out-of-the-box ideas and creativity. If you are looking for a reliable individual who is an expert in her field, Cheryl comes to the table with all the tools.

James Hoback - L'oeil L' esprit virtual tours

" " Cheryl is an extremely knowledgeable person in marketing, especially in the area of Internet. She is positive and proactive. Her abilities would be a plus for any company to have on board.

Tison King - DR Horton

" *Cheryl is 100% on the ball 24/7. She is very connected and task oriented. If she says it will be done then it will be done and it will be done when she says it will be done. She is very creative ad will take you in the direction that you want to go as long as you are creative too. I recommend her to anybody.*

James Rector - Image 360 Virtual Tours

" *I'm constantly being bombarded with online offers to increase traffic to my website and usually there is some form of scam involved. Cheryl has taught me more about SEO and Social Networking than any of these companies could teach; and I'm quite certain, saved me a ton of money!*

Suzanne Roy Director of Social Media & Industry Outreach at Move, Inc

I have worked with Cheryl in several facets of my business as a virtual assistant, including the restructure and design of my website, SEO and social networking. Cheryl is HIGHLY knowledgeable within each of these areas, along with being extremely connected. I have not only hired Cheryl in my own business, but hired people within her network of providers (two this past month alone!) - I trust Cheryl's opinion and ethics. I have and will continue to recommend Cheryl with enthusiasm and assurance of knowing her clients will be in the BEST hands possible.

Brian Castro - Virtual Vista Virtual Tours

I recommend Cheryl, because of her outstanding ability to "Get It Done!!!"

Alex Saenger - Professional Realtor

" " *Cheryl is a fantastic marketer. Her creative thought process takes her ideas to new levels, streaming past average marketing strategies.*

Paul Goodman - Captain/firefighter City of Georgetown

" " *Cheryl is a huge asset to the team. She has provided the team with a great deal of information to get us in the right direction. Cheryl and her superior marketing techniques have helped boost my exposure and sharpen my skills with my business. Thanks for sharing your expertise!*

Gabriel Duque Owner, Virtual Florida Tours

" Cheryl is an outstanding marketing professional that shares with us all of her knowledge helping us achieve our goals in our field of business.

Melanie Powers - Owner, Powerhouse Tours

" In my experience with Cheryl, she is driven and intelligent. She has a command of marketing that extends past the traditional to the new and ever-changing world of the Internet. It has enriched my personal and professional life by being associated with her. In addition to her marketing skills she also has a very funny personality that is compelling.

Dave Hall - Vice President of Marketing, Social Media Trainer and DotNetNuke Evangelist

Cheryl has been a great resource for both my clients and myself. She has been very instrumental in helping Listing Solutions build our web presence. I would highly recommend her. Thanks Cheryl.

Lawrence McBride reVISION Marketing and Consulting

Cheryl is an amazing marketer and truly understands what it takes to "stand apart from the pack" online.

Brett Weaver- Manufacturing Engineer

During my association with Cheryl, she has worked hard to provide marketing ideas and resources for my company. She is an expert in her field. Two thumbs UP!

David Dove Real Estate Photography

Cheryl is a valuable source of networking, marketing, and business website effectiveness information for me.

Severine Huchet Owner, Lawrence Virtual Tour

Cheryl is an awesome resource for marketing questions.

George Sheldon Photography

" Cheryl is a magician with marketing. I am amazed at her programs and ideas. Her programs have helped us grow.

Claudia Jaramillo - Virtual Tour and Property Marketing Specialist

" Cheryl is very professional. She has lots of marketing knowledge and has helped me in my pursuit of ranking my website in the top of the search engines.

Renard Johnson - Creative Realty Solutions, LLC

" *Cheryl has provided me with excellent marketing material. Some of her ideas where just what I needed to get my company off on the right track. Thanks for everything Cheryl and keep up the good work.*

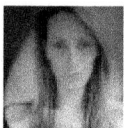

Beth Pauvlinch - Visionary Entrepreneur and Product Creator

" *Cheryl is a joy to deal with and is prompt in her responses.*

John Cobb - Realtor

" " *Cheryl is very knowledgeable in Internet marketing and provides a valuable service to people looking to advertise on the Internet and gain exposure for their business. My website traffic and leads have improved since working with Cheryl.*

Gary & Rebecca Bolda Ark-La-Tex Virtual Tours

" " *Cheryl is great! Her "out-of-the-box" marketing strategies have proven to be very effective. We have enjoyed working with her and are anticipating her future ideas will be as effective as those she has already presented.*

E.J. Domingue,Jr. Photos 2 Geaux

Cheryl is on top of her game !!!! You go girl!!!!

Keith Frank - Dream House Photography

Working with Cheryl is truly a joy. She is very personable and delivers outstanding results. Her innovative ideas are truly unique and generate a ringing phone at the business address. The value of her services cannot be overstated. While most of us lack the creativity to create eye catching material and get the market's attention, Cheryl's abilities make her the leader in the industry.

Kathy Dove - David Dove Photography

" She brought energy, enthusiasm, and leadership. Her knowledge of the Internet, which she quickly shared, has helped improve our web presence. We value her support, insights, and experience.

Alan Grochowski - Aurora Lighting LLC

" Help's me with all the things that I need for my business.

Vikki Granger - Owner, Insight360

" Cheryl is an incredible asset. Her ideas and assistance keep us all at the top of our game! We are lucky to have her as part of our team!

Charlie Nichols - NK Virtual Solutions, LLC

Cheryl does a great job developing marketing ideas. She stays in contact and passes information along on a timely basis.

Patricia Edmonds - Expressions Art and Gifts

I value the techniques and insights she brings to the table and am convinced my company's bottom line will benefit from implementing her recommendations.

Christine Kuhn - Key Solutions Virtual Tours

" *Cheryl is an effervescent, proactive achiever who is willing to share her knowledge with others. Her willingness to help others improve and learn is matched by her ability to communicate clearly and effectively. It is indeed a pleasure to work with her in any capacity.*

Beulah Parker - Indunet Solutions Virtual Tours

" *Cheryl Waller has been a big support to my company. Her marketing tools, and tips have pointed us in the right direction. We now have an effective marketing plan.*

Debra Higgins - Four Seasons Virtual Assistance

" *Cheryl is very knowledgeable in marketing and has given us great ideas for promoting our business. She is very thorough and prompt in her replies and help.*

Lance Ziegler, Co-Founder OPKsolutions.com

" *Cheryl has proven to be a great asset to the community and has proven herself a leader in marketing.*

Travis Williams - Travis Williams Construction

Cheryl deserves all seven attributes checked. (She's the best).

Elvin Clark - Independent Photography Professional

Cheryl is a highly skilled marketing consultant. She has been invaluable to me and my business. Cheryl works as a resource for me to improve web exposure for my company. I'm finding her research and her skills of communication invaluable to me and my business.

Gordon Barbosa - Cable Television Producer

"" Cheryl is someone who gets right to a task. She is diligent in helping us meet our company's needs in a timely and efficient manner. She is great to work with.

Sean Turnan - Priority Payment Systems

"" I have worked with Cheryl on and off for a few months now. Her ideas and professionalism are top notch.

Dianne Kleimola - Sneek Peek Tours, LLC of

" " *Cheryl is very much an "in charge" and "get things done" type of person. She is also very organized and detail oriented.*

Karisma Olson - Realtor at Reece and Nichols

" " *Cheryl is absolutely amazing! This woman takes a project by the horns and literally runs with it! She has the ability to think outside the box and push the limits. She exceeds any expectations that you could imagine and gives 150%, taking time to personally connect and involve everyone that she comes in contact with. Thank you Cheryl for being such a great inspiration.*

Srinivas Kopalle - Director @ Infokons LLC

" *Cheryl is talented and knows her job very well. She has very good convincing capabilities and is committed towards her work.*

Lisa Castro - Pro360 Virtual Tours & Photography

" *Since my husband and I started our Virtual Tour business we have been extremely pleased with the support and professionalism Cheryl has shown. She is always coming up with great ideas to expand our business.*

Cori Warner- Agent at Century21 Clinkenbeard Group

" *I have used the advertising campaigns, flyers, and web content provided by Cheryl. I have found her work to be creative and relevant, and have had good results with the ad campaigns. Her creativity and knowledge have helped with the successful launch of my own business. I would highly recommend Cheryl.*

Frank Nicolato - JVT Photography & Virtual Tours

" *Cheryl is, first and foremost, a professional. She knows her business, and is readily available to everyone who relies on her. I highly recommend Cheryl Waller.*

Jennifer Clark- Sales & Marketing at Total Realty Corp.

" " *Cheryl has proven to be the best in her field and I feel both comfortable and confident in her abilities to service my needs and the needs of my clients.*

Michael Basch - Virtual Access Tours

" " *Cheryl is a very responsive individual. She shows tremendous professionalism and delivers on all her promises.*

Sandra Arthur-Gibson - Power Play Multi Media Productions

" *I have had the pleasure of work with Cheryl Waller in several marketing projects to develop my niche in the real estate community. I would like to take this opportunity to recommend Cheryl as your next marketing associate.*

Chris Grumley - Anna Maria's DJ of Choice

" *Cheryl is a forward thinker, has my best interest at heart and is one to make sure that I ROCK my industry!*

SIMC

Full-Service Clients: StrategicIMcorp.com

FREE Training: GoSIMC.com

FREE Reputation Report: GetMySnapshot.com

Professional Coaching: BrassBallsUniversity.com

Publicity Advertising: TheCelebrityMakers.com

Office Hours: 9a – 5p EST Monday – Friday

(866) 986 - 5650 or (772) 237 – 3880

Support@StrategicIMcorp.com

Don't Miss Your Special Offers on Pages 196 – 200

PLUS:

Take advantage of your **Free Video Training**

GoSIMC.com

Don't Miss Your Special Offers on Pages 196 – 200

PLUS:

Take advantage of your **Free Video Training**

GoSIMC.com

10 Questions For Cheryl: Fax to (772) 934 - 7480

Chapter 1: _____

_____

Chapter 2: _____

_____

Chapter 3: _____

_____

Chapter 4: _____

_____

Chapter 5: _____

_____

Chapter 6: _____

_____

Chapter 7: _____

_____

Chapter 8: _____

_____

Chapter 9: _____

_____

Chapter 10: _____

_____

Name: _____

Business Name: _____

Email Address: _____

Contact Phone: _____

My Biggest Business Challenge: Fax to (772) 934 - 7480

_____

_____

_____

Name: _____

Business Name: _____

Email Address: _____

Contact Phone: _____